SOMEWHERE
BETWEEN HERE AND
PERFECT

2/9 2020

Carolyn—
Divine timing, mutual
gifts, energizing conversations—what a blessing
it is to have had this
time with you!
And now—open
horizons await you,
magic, joy, love,
incredibly miraculous
surprises! ♡
Lesta

I have a lot of magic coming. I will create it

Have to balance head + heart
Part of me trusts soul knows what its doing + comes in heart messages.

Drawing in magic synchronicities.
The more open to those synchronicities more they happen

Trust. that peter will be kind
Defensive energy is mirrored

All 33 year counts for everything at this point. To each of our credit that we are allowing the change to happen.

How would you like to handle it - say that alot. My attitude is i expect him to be kind + generous.

SOMEWHERE
BETWEEN HERE AND
PERFECT

Further Findings of a Fallible Free Spirit

LESTA BERTOIA

Rev. date: 12/11/2015

To order additional copies of this book, contact:
Xlibris
1-888-795-4274
www.Xlibris.com
Orders@Xlibris.com
731624

Contents

Author's note vii

Prologue ix

1   First Ring 1
2   From the Mouths of Babes 5
3   Fiber Optics 12
4   Room for More 18
5   Charades 23
6   Flying Fish 31
7   Just a Reminder 35
8   Take a Yellow Bus 40
9   The Word 44
10 Leave It to Them 52
11 Tuning Forks 58
12 Making Waves 65
13 The Artist on Loan 68
14 Their World 76
15 Filter or Non-filter 85
16 All the Same 90
17 Draggin' in Our Myths 93
18 Touch that Dial 100
19 If the Shoe Fits 105
20 Only Children 113
21 Out of the Box 117
22 Which Way? 124
23 Refreshments Are Available 132
24 Pushed and Pulled 140
25 Painted Messages 144
26 Dreamtime Travelers 150

Epilogue 155

Author's note

Much of what follows was written about 15 years ago, while I was living in Pennsylvania, with an occasional revision along the way and more recent updates to mirror the rapidly changing times. Having felt moved to pull out this old manuscript and reread the accounts and observations, I surprised myself with how much I was able to appreciate when I was 58, and how well it has served me to stay in touch with those past aspects of myself, who were also listening to this future version, the one who is now witnessing humanity approach a deeper understanding, a greater set of dimensions, and a broader sense of global family than ever before.

Here is the original introduction, as it was written then.

Prologue

I'm not sure how they do it, or who *they* are, those conspiring to ensure my sense of belonging and being recognized (angels, guardian spirits, in-between-lifers, Mr. or Ms. God, my own ingenious mind?) but they (we) did it again when I was trying to come up with a title for this book.

I'd entitled my earlier book *Somewhere between Kindergarten and God*, which was, at that moment, somewhere between having been accepted and being edited for publication.

I'd started this next book for one reason: I couldn't stop. I couldn't stop writing about the invisible beings and the people and animals that have been my marvelous mentors; about my visions and others' discoveries; about freedom and fairness and folly. Which was a good thing, because when I asked my editor, with uncontainable impatience, when my earlier book was coming out, he said he wasn't sure, but I shouldn't sit around twiddling my thumbs. Write something else, he said.

I was over halfway into this book and wondering what to call it, when I stopped at a red light and turned on the car radio. I missed the announcement about the medley that was in progress, but as I moved on with the traffic, I found myself singing along with every song fragment.

"Somewhere, my love, there will be songs to sing...

"Somewhere, over the sea, somewhere, waiting for me...

"Somewhere, over the rainbow, bluebirds fly...

"There's a place for us, somewhere a place for us..."

Each time I sang the word *somewhere*, I felt like crying. That I can't hold a tune might have had something to do with it, but I was also crying for joy, and for sadness. The message felt so personal, a timely confirmation of my other title. And it felt so universal, a message about human hope. People everywhere, for such a long time, have been hoping that someday, somewhere, life will be beautiful, life will be glorious. And then it seemed like someone was saying, do more than hope. It's time to know. Someday can be now. Somewhere can be here.

Just because our news reporters are only now catching on doesn't mean there isn't at least as much good news as bad. Just because they aren't always reporting it doesn't mean it isn't happening. Peace forums and meditation groups and consciousness-raising speakers are creating good-news-worthy events all around the world. Bookstores from Sweden to Australia are considered incomplete if they're not carrying volumes of the good news, on angels, spiritual awakening, the wisdom of the ancients, transformation, conversations with God, quantum healing, global healing, chicken soup for every soul, ways to bring abundance and love and joy and wholeness into our lives. Movies are spreading the word. Communities all over the globe are disclosing ancient secrets as well as sharing breakthrough revelations about our natural birthright as enlightened multi-dimensional beings. An astonishing percentage of American adults comprise a growing cultural force engaged in self-actualization, social evolution, ecological integrity, and spiritual awareness. As we cultural creatives, as sociologist Paul Ray calls us, grasp the significance of our numbers, our quiet but profound influence will continue to transform our society, our lives, and our world.

I thought of calling this book *Somewhere Is Here*. But it doesn't take much looking around to notice that even though we are emerging with unprecedented connectedness and momentum into a balanced world of abundance and respect for all, we are still a far cry from perfection.

We may not be able to reach perfection. I suspect that we're on this planet for other reasons: not only to acknowledge our differences, but to *be* the differences; to experiment with the creativity demanded by the challenges of our otherness; to find out who we are by exploring the distance between our realities and our ideals; to summon, from our greatest potential, the evolving actuality of a dynamic, cooperative global family. Perfection suggests a static, if lovely, absoluteness beyond the ongoing challenges of mundane life, an escape or a respite from constant change, a nice and even necessary place to visit but almost impossible to live in, considering how much the world requires our involvement and bombards us with input. Perfection is an eternal goal, and while we already exist in an eternal perfection, we're also still here. As long as here has this much light in it, this much promise, I'd rather see room for growth and improvement ahead, I'd rather be somewhere between here and perfect.

In the chapters of this book, my children show up, along with other masterful teachers, including bullfrogs, flying fish, angels that travel by Greyhound, a storm, and my sister, when she left the cult she'd been with for thirteen years. Those who toss me good news from the invisible realm include a dragon, various other selves, several Light Beings, and a friendly local goddess. Some of the subjects I've explored are quantum evolution, the binary language of time and timelessness, human beings as the Word, the dial of perception, the power of transformation, Dreamtime communications, and the artist on loan to ethereal entities.

Each one of us can share our own version, adjust our own vision, and see to it that our starting point, our present moment on the journey somewhere between here and perfect, is well worth being excited about and grateful for. Our world will be all the better for our having done so.

1

First Ring

In the movie *The Last Wave*, Richard Chamberlain, as a white-culture Australian, finds himself having disturbingly strange dreams... or are they visitations, or prophecies? In one of the dreams, he is approached by a youthful, intense-looking aboriginal man, who hands him a stone, a triangular stone with rounded corners which fits into his palm and is engraved with three concentric circles. A few scenes later, he encounters the same young man in reality, near his home, and is handed the same stone he had been given in the dream, a flat, triangular stone engraved with three circles nested within one another. Meanwhile, an aboriginal elder stalks Chamberlain in the shape-shifter form of an owl, while visions of transformation by water foretell the coming of an immense tsunami that washes over the Australian coast.

It was 1987, and I was being introduced for the first time, by this dramatic film, to prophetic messages of change. The disquieting and intriguing imagery of the film, especially the symbols of stone and owl, triggered an awareness of some resonance, some untapped mystery, inside me. Wondering what was being shifted in my sense of reality, I took a walk the next day to ponder some still unformed but vaguely insistent questions. From my sister's house outside of Boulder, Colorado, I ambled along a country road to the rim of a hill dotted with scraggly shrubs and tufts of dry grass. I descended the slope, my leather shoes crunching footprints into the parched, crusted soil, and headed through the heat to the only patch of shade beneath a lone stunted pine. I sat down on a few scattered pine needles and began to contemplate the impact of my first exposure to these mystifying suggestions of Dreamtime, an unfamiliar realm that seemed to permeate my suddenly loose-around-the-edges understanding of reality from somewhere just beyond my normal senses.

How can I learn more about Dreamtime? Can I find someone to guide me into it? Is there some way I can enter it on my own?

My questions were not framed in words. They were a vague but urgent musing, a longing. I didn't really know what I was asking. Nor did I consciously notice that shortly after I sat down, my attention was being paged – alerted as if by some unspoken whisper -- until I found myself turning to look over my left shoulder toward the base of the pine's knobby trunk.

Half sunk into the gritty dirt lay a stone about the size of my hand. I picked it up and examined it, frowning curiously at its oddly familiar shape, a roughly rounded triangle. When I turned it over and brushed it off, my eyebrows shot up. Around the center was outlined, in a different color, a circle. A single circle.

The first ring of Dreamtime! I heard myself thinking. A prickling sensation zoomed up into the roots of my hair as I clutched the stone to my chest and wondered what was happening. I wanted to meditate immediately on this propitious find, this stone that was so similar to the one I had just seen in the movie, but a large fly started buzzing annoyingly around my ears. Shooing the fly away, I got up, brushed myself off, and, holding on to the stone, trudged back up the slope and retraced my steps along the country road. At the edge of my sister's back yard, I ducked into a secluded spot within a small grove of sumacs.

With the stone in my lap, I closed my eyes, and I disappeared, or so it seemed, for even though I was vaguely aware of time having passed, I didn't know where I'd been, or for how long. I knew only that I was suddenly very aware of looking for my body. *Where's my body?!* Disoriented by the lapse in time, I darted frantically to where I'd found the stone, under the little pine tree. *My body's not here!* In a flash that was not measurable in standard time, I raced up the slope and flew along the road toward the sumacs in the back yard. As I did so, I was both a single point of perception, like the eye of a camera speeding over the blurring ground, and a spherical awareness observing the entire scene from some height above it.

In a moment that was longer than it takes to tell it and also the merest fraction of a second, I jolted back into my body with a gasp. My eyes flew open. I took a deep breath and settled into myself in the mottled shade of the sumacs.

Whew. That was *weird!*

Still shaken by the unfamiliar sensation of having lost track of my body, I studied the strange stone in my lap, but I was distracted by a tiny movement in front of me, about a foot from my crossed legs. I peered at it. I wasn't quite sure what I was looking at. A miniature owl? Two black-ringed, bright yellow eyes seemed to be staring at me from atop a soft brown body, but it was only three inches tall. The movement stirred again within the shadows of the sumacs. Finally I made sense of it. It was the slow partial opening of a pair of wings. Butterfly wings. It was a butterfly, unlike any I had ever seen before, sitting before me, catching my eye with a slight movement and then holding perfectly still so I could see the owl-like features outlined on its folded wings.

Resting my hands on the circle-marked stone, I gazed, breathlessly silent, at what I was quite sure was not a shape-shifter, at what I sensed with tingling certainty was an ineffable, invisible *something* communicating with me by using the most vividly meaningful images immediately available -- a *Presence* responding to my longing and inviting me to notice that I had indeed just entered the first ring of Dreamtime.

Although I didn't remember anything of where I'd been during what turned out to be about half an hour, I knew I'd been somewhere. If that fly hadn't chased me from where I'd found the stone, I probably wouldn't have found myself traveling that extra distance intensely aware of looking for my body. I would have simply opened my eyes thinking I'd blanked out for a moment. I wouldn't have thought to check the time, wondering how long I'd been gone. I wouldn't have seen the owl-butterfly in addition to the stone, a double confirmation of a Dreamtime conversation in symbols.

Even the fly had been part of the answer to my longing.

Which puts a whole new perspective on a lot of annoying interruptions and distractions!

Having been answered on the first ring, I continued to call. Who was doing the calling and who was being called? Yes. That, too, wanted a whole new perspective.

It wasn't until after many more such experiences, during which I was determined to stay with the part of myself that left, that I began to regard my return to my body as being similar to squeezing myself into a diving suit with a one-eyed mask.

While I'm in this wetsuit, I have to crane my neck to see what's all around me. I barely have peripheral vision, let alone my natural spherical perception that views from all angles, all distances, and all time frequencies at once. I can't directly feel the flow of the oceanic reality of pure energy through which I'm swimming, let alone taste the subtle currents with my natural body, hear the ethereal shapes of other beings around me, or see the field of light from which everything is formed. In order to participate in this denser reality, I need to maintain this suit and figure out how to readjust the gauges whose original settings reflect a lot of limitations that I'm outgrowing.

It was a relief to be reminded that I don't have to confine my awareness to what I can perceive from inside this suit. I'm looking forward to the day that I can just breathe underwater. Forget the bulky backpack and the zipless rubber! If that last wave is going to rip me right out of my wetsuit of limited and limiting experience, rip me, tsunami, I'm ready!

Nah. Easy to be flippant, but put me back in my body, stretched out on a summer lawn, watching the Milky Way float by below me to the tune of Strauss's Blue Danube, and I'm grateful that the Earth can hold me to her surface as she does. Whether it's called gravity or the curvature of space, when I'm letting go of sky-equals-up because I can remember when I saw the planet from afar and I know that sky-equals-down is just as true, I call it attachment. The Earth must be attached to me, after all, and maybe even need me, the way she keeps my body from falling outward into space. I can appreciate her attachment. I wouldn't care to have too many of my cells flying off in all directions as if they weren't part of why I exist in this reality. So, whether or not she needs to shrug until tsunamis roar, I'm enjoying what time we do have together.

We've meanwhile exchanged more than one ring.

2

From the Mouths of Babes

One afternoon, when my firstborn, Eric, was three months old, he was lying on his back on the living room carpet. (People that age tend to slump over if you try to sit them up, so they do a lot of lying around. At that age, too, if you hold them up to examine a geranium, they reach out and grab a leaf with whatever fingers get there first and crumple it with intense concentration before spastically yanking the entire plant out of its pot. They get so excited about cats, they hit them. They hit themselves, as well, ricocheting off a blow from a rattle with an injured look of worry and betrayal. The body is still largely an unwieldy surprise.)

Little Eric had just grabbed the lightweight pale green knitted baby blanket that was covering him up to his waist, and when he lifted his smooth little balls of fists into the air, he noticed the blanket waving over him. He was so thrilled by this discovery, he threw his arms up over his head in delirious excitement. Being horizontal, up over his head meant that his fists, still clamped to the blanket, were touching the carpet near his ears, and suddenly he found himself cut off from the rest of the world, with something draped over his face.

He froze. It didn't go away. What was happening? With his arms still stretched taut, he started breathing at a frantic pace. The blanket didn't lift off. Uh-oh. He started kicking compulsively. Trapped! His feet went into overdrive, like some overzealous horizontal Flamenco dancer. No air! No light! Panic!

Suddenly his arms whipped back down to his sides.

Oh! Daylight!

Whew. Air.

Wow. That was close.

He heaved a tiny sigh of relief, relaxing his arms into an orchestral conductor's gentle marking of time, and looking up, noticed the blanket above him, still caught in his clenched fists, waving randomly in the air. His mouth opened in awe, and his arms flew up over his head in a burst of renewed exhilaration.

And there he was, cut off from the world again, hyperventilating and silently bucking like someone being smothered by a pillow. The sight of the thin blanket getting sucked in and out of the dent that was his mouth made me stifle a snort of hilarity. At the sound, his arms whipped down to his sides again, leaving him wide-eyed and breathless and enormously relieved. He glanced over at me. A goofy smile spread across his face, as if to say, I knew what I was doing, I was just seeing if you knew what I was doing!

I couldn't hold it in. I had to chortle. At which reaction, he grinned and lifted his arms in a two-fisted victory salute. With the blanket still clutched in both fists. Once again, arms apparently pinned over his head, he started thrashing and hyperventilating, and then his arms whipped down, and this time he had a good silent laugh, he had fooled me, all right, *someone* had thought it was scary as all get-out to be cut off from the light and the air, but who, him?

By the fourth time, he'd made the connection. Those waving arms were attached to him! He continued to entertain me until I was the one gasping for breath, a sly smile appearing from behind the blanket every time he whipped it off his face, little stockinged feet punching the air in pure pleasure at my response.

A week later, as I was dressing him to go out, for no apparent reason he suddenly burst out with his first real belly laugh. Laughter rumbled up and out of his throat like a waterfall from a cave. He chortled. He guffawed.

Well, it was about time he got the joke!

I'm finally getting the joke myself. I have done exactly the same thing, so many times, pulled the wool over my own eyes and scared myself silly, frightened by what I couldn't see or breathe in, until an act of desperation or reversal or curiosity threw off the veil between me and the light, where someone, who knew all along that I was safer than I thought, is having a good laugh.

How easily we lose that sense of being cared for, being connected, belonging, feeling sure that whoever loves us is close by. We forget that we are the ones in control of veiling ourselves. Sometimes we forget what we know, so fearsomely, that only the fear itself can trigger us into crying out for reassurance and remembrance.

My second child, my daughter Fawni, at the age of two was finding language a welcome tool with which to alleviate the frustration of having to deal with obtuse parents. She could finally explain to us that she didn't feel like having her unruly hair brushed right now. "I can do it to-later," she'd inform me, getting back to the much more important business of hammering Cheerios with her hairbrush. She could edify us with the conclusions of her scientific experiments. "Don't press your finger by the brown pen. You will get hurt if you do it." She could assist us in choosing her diet. "I don't like dose bedgibles. I fink I want some gubblegum." (Okay, wait, how does this child know about bubblegum, I narrow my eyes at her father.)

Still, sometimes we were just too obtuse for words. I should have let her flush the toilet by herself. What was I thinking? I apologized, but my oversight was unforgivable. "I wanna flush the toilet!" was the point I didn't seem to be getting, even after a repetition of the phrase for ten minutes, so I went downstairs, and for the next twenty minutes – I looked at the clock, wondering for just how long she could go on – she stood at the top of the stairs and wailed down at me, "Don't go downstairs!"

Sometimes such a bout would lead to me howling, too. "I *hate* being a mom!"

Sometimes my efforts would pay off and she'd move on to something else. Sometimes she'd wear herself out and crawl into my lap.

It was probably after such a day of frustration that I left Fawni in the house with her dad and went into my studio to center myself. I heard her crying for me, even though she loved being with her dad, as I went out the door, but I really needed to recharge my battery.

I settled into the welcome silence and lifted out of my body. Ah. I soared upward, and then outward, spherically, breaking the envelope of the speed of light, until I popped, as softly as a soap bubble, into infinite Light, no longer I but the All, blissfully unconscious of anything but Being, basking in an endless sea of serene and lovely nothingness and everythingness, the original state of divine perfection and eternal potential, a universal purity of existence.

As I returned, shrinking my perception spherically into an individual awareness again, sensing the galaxies within me, nearing the solar system, focusing toward the planet, I felt light-filled and joyful enough to radiate love toward Fawni and her father. I hovered over our property and beamed my affection toward them, picturing them both with a smile in my heart.

I returned to the house refreshed.

Bedtime had recently become our time to review special events. Sometimes Fawni recalled something we'd enjoyed during the summer, the aquarium or a little traveling circus. This evening she said to me, "'Member I was cryin' with Peter, an' you was up there, an' you was sayin' hi?" She pointed at the ceiling.

"You were crying with Peter, but then you were okay again?"

"Yes." She nodded.

"I was meditating in the studio," I told her.

"You was in the studio, an' you was up there." She pointed at the ceiling again. "An' you was sayin' hi."

"Up there?" I asked.

She looked a little embarrassed for me. "Mm-hm," she said, waiting.

"You mean outside?" I was suddenly getting what she was telling me.

"Yes! Outside, in the sky." She was obviously pleased.

"Yes, I *was* up there." I was thinking fast now. "Sometimes I feel like I'm flying. Did you ever feel like that?"

"Mm-hm. Like a arrow," she told me. "Up and up, and den down." A few weeks ago, she had seen an arrow released into the sky for the first time. She'd finally acquired a word, and I'd finally asked her a question, that enabled her to describe her experience to me.

It occurred to me that our departures into our other perceptual dimensions weren't in synch. During the last couple of weeks, whenever I had tried to meditate in the house, to go on a mini-vacation from this reality, I had had to come back, because I'd hear Fawni crying pitifully to her dad, "I want Mama! I want Mama!"

"Fawni, whenever I meditate and go up into the sky, I will only be gone for a few minutes, and I will always come back to be with you. Okay?"

She snuggled close.

"Okay?" I wanted to be sure she felt reassured.

"Mm-hm." She was drifting off to sleep, content.

She was never again upset when I would go off to meditate.

It's such a delicate quality, this sense of being connected. It's so easy to feel we're losing it. It's so easy to learn to steel ourselves, to endure isolation even while we crave connection and grab at every passing straw, more money, more food, false intimacy, fame. It's no wonder we respond with hope to the news that angels are among us, that our higher selves are guiding us, that the universe is abundantly in love with us. We think it's news, anyway, because in our fear of losing what we have, we don't allow ourselves the time to be assured that we have never lost what is truly ours. In our excitement about what we're capable of doing, we cut ourselves off from what is always with us. It isn't really news, of course -- it's as old as the universe itself, this connection, this belonging, this being part of everything.

It's easy to forget, though, it seems to me, because that's exactly why we've come here, to forget. We have chosen to immerse ourselves into this life on Earth so that we can know the otherness of separation, and, having known it, we can know the hilarity that rises in our being when we toss away the veil, we can know the warm contentment of belonging when we surrender to the truth. We have entered this reality of three-plus-one dimensions to experience a specific spectrum. We've become prismatic, dividing the light that we are into all these many colors. In the density of gravity and matter, social law and separate skins, we learn to alternate our frequencies, to switch ourselves on and off so we can discern the disparities between this state and that. We're here to be the differences.

We're here to forget, but, then, too, we're here to remember. Angels *are* among us. Children are our teachers. Our future selves embrace us. Spirit lives within us. Light is what we're made of.

We remember by increasing our vibrations.

My daughter had been aware of me leaving my body. She had lowered the vibrations of her soul awareness, not so much that she couldn't sense me, but enough to fear that I could disconnect from her. She continued to slow her frequencies, with the help of the institution of education, until she was fully engaged in the trials and tribulations of boxes and grids, but shortly after graduation from high school, she began to raise them until she could again begin to sense her oneness with the ethereal realm. During a massage therapy class on energy work, while she was cupping her hands under a classmate's head, her life force quickened into euphoria. As she filled with love, she felt a pair of hands resting on her shoulders, and she heard someone whispering near her ear. "Yes, this is what you are meant to do." Thinking that her teacher had crossed the room without her noticing it, she turned around. There was no one behind her. No one human, anyway. Her teacher told her later that she could see a host of healing spirits around Fawni.

Gradually Fawni experienced her energy work with her clients as a merging with various parts of their bodies. She would become the organ or the muscle, become its voice, give it the energy it asked for and translate its message to her client. She was at that time an intuitive healer, consciously conducting the energy she could invite in from the invisible realm. She has since found her intuition to have access to many layers of information, emotional and spiritual as well as physical, and has begun to teach others to tune into and trust that inner receptivity to a pertinent truth.

It has taken her and many of her generation, it seems to me, much less time than it took me and mine -- to make the descent into the vibrations of matter, culture, institutions, conflicts, social demands, and to begin the ascent again into a remembrance of all the liberating and intriguing frequencies available to us.

That remembrance is contagious. There's an epidemic. Humanity is dying to live in a vaster set of dimensions, but we're discovering that we don't have to shed our bodies to do it.

Michael Talbot reports in *The Holographic Universe* the merging of science, particularly in the field of quantum physics, and mysticism, which sees this apparently solid reality as an illusion, a convincing dream concocted by Consciousness. At the level of quantum wave-particles, there is only an infinite field of interacting frequencies. Scientifically, what our senses seem to perceive is actually the interference patterns of the vibrating flowing space that we are made of with the vibrating flowing space that surrounds and permeates us. Mystically, we are all facets of the same Dreamer, participating in the creation of experience.

Robert Scheinfeld, in *Busting Loose from the Money Game*, actually outlines, as he describes it, the process of busting loose from the Human Game. In the first phase of our lives, he says, we have immersed ourselves into and thoroughly convinced ourselves of a reality separate from us, largely beyond our control, irrevocably solid and consistent. In the second phase, he suggests, we begin to get messages from the true self, the ultimate Dreamer. We find ourselves gradually clued in to our amazing creative acuity. We begin to understand that it is not this personality-self, this dream character, but the Creative Consciousness that is the ultimate Self, who is writing the story, designing the game.

My introduction to Dreamtime through the discovery of a symbolic language showing up in the form of a circled stone and a butterfly with owl's eyes on its wings excited me at the age of 43. Five years earlier, however, I had overheard my two-and-a-half-year-old daughter, who was enjoying a bath while I was putting away folded towels in the hall closet, singing to herself. Already then I was being prepared to get the bigger picture as I listened to her words: "We are all so conscious, but we like to play along. *Now* I know what time to do. *Now* I know what *time* to do! I know myself. I know myself."

3

Fiber Optics

At a moment of feeling disconnected myself, or feeling disconnected from my Self, I took a walk from my earth-sheltered house in Pennsylvania, turned right at the end of my long gravel driveway, and headed down the hill on a country road bounded by fields and forests on either side. I had no pressing problem that needed solving, no question about what decision would best serve everyone involved. I was simply hoping, from a place of emptiness, for some indication that I was still somehow noticed by whatever greater Awareness had seemed available to me before.

The weather was cooling, autumn was approaching, and a delicate breeze gently swayed the goldenrod, asters, and cornflowers that edged the fields and pine groves. Being outside was treat enough to make me forget my mission, so I turned around at the crossroads a quarter of a mile away and headed for home, already feeling better, when something caught my eye. Floating toward me from across an open field was a tiny parachuted milkweed seed, its little brown oval carried by soft white fibers into the air above me. I watched it, becoming mesmerized as it circled slowly about ten feet over my head, a full circle of about 12 feet in diameter, and then, as I stopped walking and continued to watch, it followed the same circular pattern again, and then, again, for the third time, it made a complete circle overhead. I stood in the middle of the road, my eyes fastened on this phenomenon, my thoughts silenced into a mode of receptivity, and the milkweed seed floated down toward my face and attached itself to the space between my eyebrows, over the area known as the third eye.

Now I am standing perfectly still, holding my breath and noticing that as I look through the luminous filaments perched between my eyes, the light seems to change. Everything looks brighter. The landscape seems somehow to be made of light. Which, of course, I suddenly remember, it is. I am alone on a country lane, gazing through these exquisitely fine organic threads at a light-filled world, and… I get it! I've been told my need for reassurance was heard. I've been answered. I've been shown what I needed just now to know. I'm silently dropping my jaw and laughing and saying thank you and wow, and when I whisper, "I get it!" the little milkweed parachute detaches itself, lifts off, and floats away.

I continue walking, but I am no longer looking at tangible trees and dryly rustling cornstalks. I am seeing the intersection of energy and imagination, I am viewing the lucid dream created by the interactions among the spectrum of electro-magnetic waves as interpreted by my senses, which are also merely quantum vibrations, and my mind explodes open. I get it even more so: there is nothing here but different rates of motion, interfacing ripples of emanations, the miraculous dream of Consciousness observing itself through itself divided. I am as a wave of water is to the ocean, continuous with it, indistinguishable and yet observably separate, for a moment in time, and time is the basic and essential instrument of manifestation, time measured in frequencies is how the void of infinite potential becomes the Universe of unending versions of reality. This that I am witnessing is as much an extension of myself as I am an extension of it.

I reach the driveway and I'm still marveling at the sensation of solidity beneath my feet, at the nuances and varieties of color, at the lifting of my hair by a breeze, all this is pure energy interpreted by the pure energy that is me. I am in awe of the artistry, what an intelligent-beyond-comprehension creation, what a supremely exquisite display of what can be done with frequency, with time. And who or what is the doer doing this that has been done? There is a sense of a You and an I overlapping, an Otherness seeking to be witnessed and experienced by Itself who is made up of me and them and that and this and those and you. I explode again. This is My Dream. I explode again. I am being Dreamed. Infinity is endless both beyond Me and within Me, a forever-unfolding mystery, and this me walking along this driveway is tearful with joy, completely connected, and totally in love.

It wasn't until much later that I watched the neuroanatomist Jill Bolte Taylor's online video, A Stroke of Insight, during which she described the onset of her own stroke and triggered yet another revelation for me. While the left side of her brain, the side that enables us to coordinate walking and talking, was shutting down, the right side was noticing what I had noticed on my walk: she couldn't discern where "she" ended and "out there" began. She felt expansive, euphoric, and utterly peaceful, until the hemorrhaging side of her brain told her, hey, we have a problem, we need help! Because of the switching, it became even clearer to her than it had been during her years of research as a brain scientist that the two parts of the brain serve entirely different purposes. The left side is linear, past-and-future-oriented, thinks in language, goes over details, categorizes and plans. It is the choreographer of our personal, interactive, daily lives, the side of the self that says I exist, I am, I am a separate being. The right side thinks in images, exists in the vast present moment, absorbs all information as perfect and beautiful energy, experiences connectedness to everything, knows itself to be one with Nirvana, and is the witness of the other self.

My mind popped: we are equipped with two organs of organizing perception -- we are able to interpret and experience a solid three-dimensional reality with one of our brains, and an infinite field of energy with the other, and *we have both of these instruments inside our crania because both of these realities are there to be perceived.* One brain fully immerses us into the focal range of the manifest world and enables us to have a human experience. The other zooms us into a multi-dimensional sea of frequency interactions, connectedness, and creative comprehension, giving us a glimpse into the transcendent state of Oneness.

Somehow the arrival of the milkweed seed had moved my focus of attention completely into my right brain, and almost as if I had removed a pair of dark glasses, I could see what wasn't noticeable with the glasses on, the truly brilliant colors of the world. Shifting back into my left brain's way of perceiving reality was similar to putting the dark glasses back on to change my reception of what was awesome and inspiring but also distracting enough by virtue of its brilliance to hamper functioning as a responsible human being.

An emphasis on left-brain perception insists on an unconscious and objectifiable world separate from ourselves, and it has made possible many technological advances, some of which are beneficial, and some not, to humanity. The awareness interpreted by the right brain is labeled in various ways (Divine Source, the Tao, Great Mystery, Universal Consciousness, God, etc.) and is magical and awe-inspiring but not practical and also prone to being misused. Either alone is as incomplete and disabling as having only one of two other body parts (eyes, lungs, kidneys, legs, hands); we can still function, but not as fully, fluidly, and freely as when we are able to make use of both. Either alone is an imbalance not as amenable to healthy life as is a cooperation between the two.

An example of bringing both perspectives into playful, magical, useful, and informative balance is the work done by the Japanese scientist Dr. Masaru Emoto with water crystals. He discovered that water reacts to thoughts, emotions, intentions, music, prayer, ambience, even to written words taped onto the vial in which it is contained. Countless images recorded in the volumes entitled *Messages in Water* show samples of water droplets purposefully influenced and then photographed under a microscope at the moment of being frozen. The results demonstrate, for instance, that water from a bottle labeled Love produces a perfectly symmetrical and beautifully complex six-pointed star-shaped crystal, while water from a bottle labeled Hate produces an incomplete and disorganized crystal. Water exposed to Beethoven shows up as a perfectly formed multi-layered symmetrical crystal; water exposed to hard metal rock music is disjointed and murky in its frozen state. Water taken from a polluted lake and frozen under the microscope had no resemblance to a crystal at all; water taken from the same lake after 300 people had prayed over it produced crystals as exquisitely intricate and symmetrical as a snowflake. One of the results I found most intriguing was the difference between water set next to a computer being used by a person who was resistant to what he was seeing, uncomfortable with the information he was reading, and water sitting next to someone who was using the computer creatively and was enjoying the process. The first, an off-center and incomplete crystal, in contrast to the second, another perfect rendition of beauty, proved that the computer itself is a neutral influence; it is the choice and reaction of the user that determines how a large percent of the body's makeup resonates and aligns itself on a molecular level within the cells and bloodstream of the human being.

It occurs to me that Emoto's breakthrough observations are one way in which the balanced access of both brains harmonizes what we can learn about our world, how we can improve it, how we can participate in the transformation of idea and desire into layers and levels of curiosity and interaction and love made tangible and visible. There are probably seven billion degrees of availing ourselves of the information we humans receive and project from the processing of incoming frequencies. As an artist and an empath, I tend to flow easily into an intimacy with the Great Mystery to give meaning and depth to my life, while generating an income or using a simple cell phone are somewhat daunting demands on my senses. I have a friend who is a skilled surgeon and corporate administrator who nevertheless listens to his dreams, applies mythology to his life journey, and is open to a re-enchantment of the world too long objectified by science. Perhaps we can hope for, strive for, and educate ourselves toward the eventual cooperative partnership between the halves of the brains of every individual on the planet, thereby recreating a world of compassionate recognition of ourselves and all earthly life as intricately and dynamically connected not only to our home in the solar system but to the entire cosmos. And in the meantime, let us appreciate that the Conscious Beingness, of which each of us is a holographic point of focus, is experiencing itself, discovering itself, and recreating itself through this immeasurably astonishing diversity of light-sculpted realities contributed to by each and every dreamed and dreaming version of itself. Which is to say, to my way of seeing it (through the luminous fibers of a milkweed seed), no matter how imperfect it appears from one point of view, from another, it's already perfect. Somewhere between here and perfect is the length of a synapse.

Having learned the symbol of a little floating seed parachute as a message from the otherwise Invisible, I was now equipped to be better communicated with, as I discovered when my daughter and I had cleaned out the Pennsylvania house prior to selling it. We'd separated the keeps and the donates, and sat on the lawn at the end of the day, exhausted, viewing with misgivings the rather large pile of discarded trash. "How are we going to get this much stuff to the dump?" Fawni wondered, reasonably enough, as we had no access to a pickup truck. I had no ready answer, but out of the corner of my eye I saw a milkweed seed come floating toward us from the nearby field. It approached the pile of trash bags and broken objects, and touched down lightly in two places — picture an invisible fairy godmother with her magic wand marking the object of transformation. "Did you see that?" I asked my daughter. She did. "We don't have to worry," I found myself saying. And the next morning we both laughed with delight and gratitude when a neighbor from down the road pulled up in his pickup truck and asked, "Anything I can do to help?"

There were other instances. In response to a shift in attitude that I knew was the more responsible reaction to a certain situation, I was granted a confirmation. I'd been waiting for the light to change, tapping the steering wheel as I realigned my thoughts. Just as I altered them from worry and concern to trust and gratitude, a seed parachute crossed the windshield outside, from right to left, turned the corner into the open window next to me, and settled on the dashboard. My mouth dropped open, and then I cheered inside. Thank you!

I was recently describing this series of events to three friends sharing a table with me in a restaurant on Maui. We were seated in a large room with a wall of windows open to the balmy breezes, but it was from the inner depths of the closed-in area that a white puff of fibers floated toward us, sailed over my shoulder, skidded across the table, and bumped up against the arm of the one woman least likely to wrap her mind around what I was saying. "What?!!" she exclaimed. "Are you kidding me? There are no milkweed pods on Maui. I've lived here for seventeen years and I have never seen anything that looks like this." The rest of us just sat there, electrified, grinning, and finally chattering away like a flock of mynah birds. One of us had just been shown that there's another kind of language.

4

Room for More

I am inside my heart. The softly glowing, warm red walls of a curving corridor are pulsing gently on either side of me. I am standing barefooted on a resilient floor, beside a feature in the inner wall, a slit through which shines a hint of light. My hand, raised to feel it, slips through, so I ease myself into what appears to be a chamber. In a dreamy space that seems much bigger than my heart, I see my children, my siblings, my parents, my mates, my friends, all the people I have ever taken into my heart. They are all still here. There are more of them than I remembered.

Over there is a little boy of about three I met only once. He and I played bang-you're-dead-oh-you-got-me in a boutique in Santa Barbara, while his nanny, who called his name occasionally to make sure he was behaving, did her shopping. I was just browsing, waiting for my friend Fran to choose something for herself.

"I don't think you want to buy these shoes." Jonathan had crept out from under a rack of clothes and picked up a pair of pink plastic sandals.

"Oh? Why not?"

"Because they're *green*." He wrinkled his nose.

"You're right." I wrinkled my nose, too. "I don't want to buy them."

Alternating with having to present himself to his nanny, he continued to emerge from between dresses on racks to offer me astute suggestions that made me giggle. I didn't see him anywhere when Fran and I left the store, so I called out, "'Bye, Jonathan! Have a good life!"

18

Fran and I were halfway up the block when I heard, "Wait!" I turned around, and Jonathan was running toward me. I swept him into my arms and swung him around, and he hugged me tightly. As his nanny hurried toward us, I whispered, "Thank you!" He waved to me over her shoulder, but even though they disappeared into the store again, he must have left himself, fifteen minutes of himself at the age of three, inside my heart.

There sits a man whose name I don't know, an elderly man who sat beside me in a counseling group I attended after my first divorce. I was a single mom, lonely, scared, and withdrawn, but I didn't think it showed. I didn't want it to show. I never saw him look at me, but he reached over, silently wrapped his hand around mine, so that our forearms were touching, and gently patted it as we listened to the speaker, as if it were precious, as if I were precious, as if he knew me better than I knew myself. I had never known, and I was thirty-one, that a simple human touch could feel so deeply comforting and reassuring. I don't even remember what he looked like, but here he is, inside this chamber in my heart.

There sits a young man, a musician who put an ad in the paper looking for a babysitting job. Two evenings a week, as soon as Clint arrived, little Eric would tell me, "You can go now, Mom, 'bye, have a fun time." When I came home from my counseling group, Eric would tell me all the things they'd done together, and then as my little boy fell asleep on the couch between us, Clint would stay, way past the hours for which he would let me pay him, and let me talk, single-mom-me, until I, too, was sleepy. He had so much room in his heart. I wish I could tell him, as he sits there playing his guitar, what a wonderful man Eric has become.

There's Mrs. Raymond, my seventh-grade English teacher, telling me that I could be a writer someday. She was the only person who ever said that to me when I was young. And there's Mrs. Asquith, my eighth-grade history teacher, who during activities period braided my hair and whispered conspiratorially to my only girl friend, another self-consciously shy thirteen-year-old, that she, too, liked people like me better than she did people like so-and-so, naming a popular girl in school. I loved her for that.

There's my senior-year English teacher. Wait a minute, what's he doing in here? I thought I despised him! He decided that we college-bound students needed several weeks' review of fifth-grade grammar. He explained subjects and predicates, to our unbelieving ears, as if we were foreigners, dividing noun from verb with exaggerated sweeps of his arms, the butterfly stroke of sentence structure. It was his secret desire, we were convinced, to flunk us all -- he gave us A-F quizzes on the literature we were reading (one wrong was an F), and on each quiz was one question that we hadn't covered in class, like, what was Shakespeare's true love's mother's maiden name?

One day we wore paper balls-and-chains around our ankles, shuffling into class for yet another hour of rolling our eyes behind his back.

He assigned each of us a day on which *we* would teach the class the material we were covering. Those who had done so before me had groaned at lunchtime that it had taken them all night to prepare, since we didn't know until a day before what our assignment would be. He stopped me in the hall one morning to tell me that since so-and-so was absent, I would be the one teaching that afternoon. I watched him walk away, with angry tears burning my eyes at how unfair he was.

So when did he slip into this chamber in my heart? Several of us seniors complained to the head of the English department. He did not come back the following year. Word got around that he'd had a nervous breakdown. And for a moment, my heart must have opened, just the tiniest bit, just enough to let him in, for there he is, pulling compassion from my observing eyes, possibly a distraught and lonely gay man in a sixties' high school.

And there's Mr. Neiman, my senior math teacher, who, seeing me crying in the hallway, told me I could use his math class to prepare for teaching English that afternoon. With one small act of kindness, he restored my faith in human beings.

I see so many people in here, more than I can count. I'm so happy that I've found them all in here, and, knowing that they'll be here, any time I want to look again, I slip back out into the corridor.

Running my hand along the smooth warmth of the gently pulsing wall, walking barefoot on the fleshy floor, bathed in a soft red glow, I notice another hint of light, another slit. I slip through the opening. Inside this chamber, I find myself looking at a beautiful spherical world of blue and white, floating in space. Oh, well, of course, I should have known I'd find her in my heart, her and her entire family of living beings, not only those nestled close, the animals and plants, the creatures of the sea, the rocks and clouds, but those other members of her family, the sun and planets, and her distant relatives, the stars. I can't remember how many times my heart has opened to take them all in, looking at a photograph of Jupiter, feeling the sun on my shoulders, being greeted by a gentle giraffe in a drive-through park, waving to a family on a canal in Thailand, watching meercats on PBS, standing in awe beneath a natural arch of red-gold stone, getting drenched in a thunderstorm, catching sight of a glowing meteor plunging to earth. This chamber seems to have no walls. I could lose myself in here. I can come here any time, to do exactly that.

I follow the curving corridor around the inner chambers, curious about what else I'll find in this heart of mine. Haven't I already found it all? But here's another glowing entrance. I slip inside. It's so bright in here, my eyes need to adjust. What am I looking at? Shimmering, floating essences. Are they fairies? Angels? Guardian spirits? There in the background is a crystalline city. I remember coming here, in my dreams. I remember being led into a room full of books, the records of my lives. Some of them were thin, others rather hefty. I pulled one from the shelf and saw a bookmark in it, so I knew how much of this life I had already written.

Aha, this must be where my imagination and the invisible reality interface. (If hearing and sight are created by the interference patterns of the frequencies that we and our holographic environment are made of, then isn't imagination also a sense, one that relays to us what the others do not?) This chamber is where I can learn to understand and love even more than I can with my physical senses. Yes, there, I see, more of my visions, my inspirations and aspirations. This is where I first saw my largest painting. I couldn't wait to put it on canvas. This is where I've met my future self. This is where I can come to refine the use of my third eye. The host of healing spirits that her teacher saw hovering around my daughter Fawni, I could learn to see them here. They're in my heart. I love them for being Fawni's helpers. The angels whose presence we have felt when any of my friends has prayed for guidance or help, the ethereal essences of souls not in bodies, the forms taken by messengers in my dreams, even others' visions, Black Elk's, Vivaldi's, Rudolph Steiner's, Graham Hancock's, are in this chamber. Oh, my, I don't want to leave. I feel so much love and inspiration and abundance in here. I'm so glad I can come back whenever I want to.

I turn around, slip myself through the pliable opening in the pulsing wall, and listen to the gentle thud-thud, thud-thud as I walk along, bathed in a vermilion glow.

Within the next chamber I see me, every moment of this lifetime so far. I don't have to wait until I die for a life review. I can look at everything I've ever done, right here in my heart, and because of how it feels to be in here, I can love it all, even though I was so often foolish, hurtful, even cruel. As I stand in here, looking at that little girl, that young woman, that midlife-crisis maniac, this post-menopausal crone, I can see that as I embrace all of my aspects, all of my moments, I can live the rest of my life with all of them inside me, nestled in my heart.

Well, let me see, that was four chambers, but what's this, another entrance? What's in here? Oh, hi, great Cosmic Birther! Mind at large, Consciousness, quantum foam, Allah, Tao, Self, Dreamer, Universe, God, Great Mystery. Look at all those names and faces giving creative form to Light and Love!

Okay, so, have I come full circle yet? I better check into this next one to see. Oh, my. This is where I harbor all the suffering of the world. All the anguish, all the sadness, all the grief. Right here in my heart. Now I know why it hurts so much sometimes. It must be connected to all these other hearts throbbing with what else this life is still about. This is where I make my vow to ease the pain by balancing its weight with joy.

Is this it, then? Yes, this next chamber looks like the first... no, wait. There are people in here, but I don't recognize them. I can't even see their faces, really. Who are these people? People I haven't met yet! They're already in my heart? Oh, it's good to know this room is here. Always room for more.

5

Charades

When I discovered, years ago, that I could visit my future self in that chamber in my heart where my imagination interfaces with the invisible realm, I did so fairly often. I would approach her, on the beach or in a marble-columned temple, a much older woman, older even than I am now, with a long gray braid hanging down her back, wearing a long, loose, unbleached-cotton dress, and I would study her serene countenance, the contentment in her smile, the amusement in her eyes, and I would ask her, how? How can I be like you? How can I ever turn out like you when I'm in this mess, when I've made all these mistakes, when I can't see my way through the brambles, when I'm so overloaded and losing my mind and taking it out on the kids? She wouldn't say anything. She would just smile. And shrug. As if to say, I'm here. You'll get here. And that would make a lot of sense. I would feel comforted.

She was right. I am getting there. Slowly.

If she could visit with me, if my seventy-something self could visit with my forty-something self and toss her a lifeline with which to haul herself out of the swamp, did my thirty- or forty-something self visit an even younger me?

Yes! A moment pops into my mind at once, one I have visited again and again, from many different ages. And each visit, from each more mature age, as I see it now, granted even more to that little girl I once was. The first few times I went back there, I didn't give her what I can now, but now that I've been back there again, from this age, I can see that she's also been visited by an even older me.

I was eleven, and my brother Val was six, and my sister Celia was a baby asleep in her crib.

Val and I had been, for years already, unconsciously encouraged by my mother to fear our father's judgement. We harbored a lot of anxiety. My brother sucked his thumb and wet his bed. Both of us were nail-biters and nighttime teeth-grinders. My mother would have been happy to let us "grow up like weeds," as she used to say, "who turned into flowers all by themselves," but when my father was due home for dinner, we would all make a hasty appraisal of the house, putting away tossed coats or scattered toys in order to avoid a frowning mutter of disapproval.

Both parents having learned their manners in Europe, Val and I were expected to sit quietly and politely at the dinner table. (We didn't have much choice. Each of us was trapped by a parent sitting on the escape end of a high-backed bench in the booth by the kitchen window.) We were expected to clean our plates -- and we didn't get to choose how much food was put onto them -- before asking to be excused. (Years later, when all the radiators in the old stone house were replaced by baseboard heaters, something mysterious was discovered behind the one beneath the kitchen window. A two-foot-high pile of ancient, moldy, discarded food. I never saw my brother slip his heated-up canned string beans into the handy cache, and he didn't know I was sneaking my leathery bits of burnt pork chop over the side of the table. We had been individually clever in creating an extra option.)

Although we didn't want to challenge the monster which, through our mother's eyes, appeared to be waiting to spring with a frothy roar from just beneath my father's often tense demeanor, his two decades of simmering frustration and impatience (which eventually mellowed) almost never resulted in a physical or even a vocal outburst, so it was with unprecedented dread that Val and I, who were supposed to be in bed asleep, since it was after nine o'clock, overheard an actual argument in progress downstairs, a shrill feminine voice, a dark rumbling response. We crept to the grating, a heat vent in the pine floor of our shared bedroom, just in time to witness, in the dining room below, something we had never seen before: my father slapping my mother, my mother crying out, turning on her heel, and slamming the door on her way out.

We glanced at each other in the echo of the stinging slap and shuddering floorboards, appalled.

And then we heard the worst possible sound. My father's footsteps, on the stairs. He was coming upstairs! We scrambled back to our beds and dove under our covers. I panicked. I leaped up, locked the bedroom door for the first time in my life, and scuttled back into my bed, my heart pounding at my rib cage to be let out *now*.

The footsteps stopped outside the door. The door handle turned. There was a pause. The handle turned again, and the door was tested, pushed, but, of course, it didn't open.

"Val, open the door," came from the other side of the door, in a voice that was way too controlled.

Little Valdy looked at me, reluctantly edging his foot to the floor to comply. I pierced him with my older sister eyes, shaking my head no. The foot was withdrawn.

"Val," the Voice commanded, "open the door."

The foot inched out from under the covers again. I directed silent horror at its intention. It disappeared.

Suddenly the door slammed open so hard it crashed against the wall and bounced back against a shoe, from the sound of it, although I hadn't seen it, for I had turned and whipped over my head what felt like an impossibly thin sheet of protection between me and the wrath of the household god.

The side of my bed sagged under a weight, and my stomach dove for the basement, expecting a blow that would sting for all eternity, for having locked him out, for having forced my brother to disobey him. There was a monster, after all, just beneath the controlled exterior. It had just assaulted my mother.

What I felt instead was a hand placed gently on my shoulder.

Under the covers, I stared through the space in front of my eyes, listening, feeling, swallowing. I had to do something. In the echo of the slap on my mother's cheek, anger and sorrow and the desire to admonish him darkened my heart. But could I summon the courage to scowl at him? I had never been anything but expressionless in the face of his impatience and criticism. No, despite the gentleness of the waiting hand, I was afraid. I was powerless. I turned over, slowly, coming up from under the sheet, and dared a cautious look at my father.

I was dumbfounded. On his face was an expression I had never seen there before. He was worried and confused. He was hurting. He was in pain.

My heart rushed toward him, hungry to surround him with comfort and love. But my eleven-year-old self didn't know how to express to my heretofore emotionally self-sufficient father what I was seeing and feeling. So I didn't say anything. I didn't move.

"Lesta," he said, and he said my name so infrequently that some part of me stowed away the rarity to treasure later, while another part felt called upon to fulfill this name that suddenly presented such a weight of responsibility, this word heavy with silent pleas. He paused. "I don't understand your mother."

This unprecedented reversal of parent-child roles flipped time on its edge, and into an eleven-year old girl, other ages of herself slipped themselves inside.

"She just wants you to believe her," I told him. I didn't pat his hand or touch his shoulder, but my voice was tender. "She isn't attracted to anyone else. She loves you. She just wants you to believe that." That was as much as I had gleaned from my mother's confidences, but then I offered what she hadn't articulated. "She just wants you to love her." He sat quietly, looking at the floor. What didn't rise into words, then, that I myself just wanted him to love me, too, didn't seem to matter. He was the one needing reassurance. "Don't worry, she'll come back," I went on. "She'll just take a walk in the woods to be by herself for a while, and then she'll come back." And I would give her the love that he couldn't. As I was giving him the love that she couldn't. How I wished that they could acknowledge and understand and express their love for one another.

He nodded. "Yes," he said. "Everything will be fine in the morning." He patted my head, went to my brother's bed and patted his head, too, and told him to go to sleep now, and then quietly closed the door behind him.

I grew up encapsulating the moments of hurt between my parents, hiding them away from myself, and welcoming the moments of contentment, the after-dinner conversations and games of chess, the brief hugs, the walks we all took together to enjoy the changing seasons. I reached my twenties convinced that my parents had loved each other and that I had had a happy childhood.

When I went back there in my late thirties, I did so with the indignation and self-pity of a victimized woman whose emotionally distant father never comforted *her*, never again took her into his confidence (not until she was an adult, anyway, but that didn't count), never again, or at least not in the years that mattered, let her know that he was only human and not the last word on the planet. I went back with anger and said, see, sweetie, this is where it all begins, this weird thing you have later about men whose pain you don't believe until they break down your door so you'll listen and then you just can't stop listening, you want so badly to make it better. This is where you start getting messed up about what you need to do for yourself, protect yourself, stand up for what *women* need. Well, it was a start, I was offering my eleven-year-old self some kind of identity, and as I see it now, it might have been my thirty-something self who prompted young Lesta to lock the door.

In my early forties I returned with a different perspective. Despite the odds against any iota of self-esteem, little girl self, you can rally and accept, for a brief moment in the spotlight, the role of comforter, and prepare yourself to comfort others, for you are being prepared, however unconsciously, by both parents, to feel responsible for others' sense of well-being. Forgive them for their ignorance and be grateful for their gifts.

As I assume it was for many others of my generation, each decade expanded into a new theme, a cultural as well as an individual one. There's a beautiful thought expressed in Marlo Morgan's *Mutant Message from Forever*. Judgement and forgiveness require one another, while observation is without an emotionally charged opposite. If I don't judge someone as the blameworthy cause of something painful, if I have merely observed what has happened, there is no need to forgive, there is no victim, and therefore no perpetrator, there are only participants in an exchange. So, too, we need to forgive or justify or identify ourselves only if we have judged ourselves, or misjudged ourselves, rather than having simply observed ourselves with neutrality or interest or understanding. This principal, this pure, simple, straightforward, basic universal law, of neither judging nor forgiving but simply observing, Morgan credits to the Aboriginal people, who seem never to have lost their direct connection to what's real. The next decade for me was one of observing, moving beyond the need for blame or forgiveness, lightening the emotional weight of my past to carry on with greater agility in my present.

Eventually I went back to give that little girl a conscious soul. She had made her own choices, ones that had landed her in a set of circumstances that would teach her to look through the masks of others and know how to respond to their pain and need.

Well, how great was that, I mumbled just last year, I've had to unlearn *that* whole lesson, people have to be responsible for themselves, you can't do their growing for them.

I know now that my little girl self has been visited by an older me as well, because not only can she experience that event as an observer, looking into the hearts and souls of each participant, understanding from where each is coming, on many levels of humanness and soul awareness at once, she can do it with a compassionate and bemused smile. She knows that her parents *do* love each other, and her. She *is* having a happy childhood.

After all, she never ate a thing she didn't want to, and she and her brother are still cracking up together about their childhood escapades.

Whenever our muffled giggles escalated into audible hilarity at bedtime, Val and I knew we were risking a thunderous "Quiet!" from our father's bedroom across the hall. We'd invented our own version of King of the Hill, a game by which we could test our skills of resistance. Each of us, while trying to stay on the bed, attempted to shove the other onto the floor (as soundlessly as possible). Partial removal didn't count, a hand still on the bed was not a win, and if the hand was removed but a foot reached the mattress, there was still some scrambling to be done, generally generating an irrepressible amount of tittering. Usually one of us would win, not by prowess, but by default, since, at the admonishment of "Quiet!" -- the third one so loud it seemed to rattle the walls -- we would have to stuff our mouths with pillow, squirming and bouncing to keep the giggles from escaping, and one of us would inevitably fall off the bed without being shoved, leaving the other a winner so overcome with hilarity that he or she was in danger of forfeiting the victory, as well as summoning not just the Voice but the Withering Eye.

Although the connection was not made consciously, we then devised a game that both honed our ability to suppress our laughter and gave us the opportunity to release it full force without threat of admonishment.

We played it when my father wasn't home, of course. It was our own version of Charades, in which the point was not to give visual signals toward the guessing of a word, but to act out a scene that would force the other to laugh, no matter how hard he or she was trying not to.

The mimed scene (and every one was different, there was never a repeat) could be introduced with a helpful description, if needed, such as, "I'm sick in bed, and the nurse who's bringing me my orange juice weighs nine hundred pounds." The patient, lying on the couch looking convincingly feverish and lethargic, begins to bounce uncomfortably at the ponderous approach of the virtual nurse, each flat-out bounce a little more uncontrollable, until the last step has lifted the wildly flailing and highly distressed patient two feet off the couch. The audience is repressing a smile, with both hands, but that doesn't count, it has to be a laugh. So the patient, exhausted and relieved to be lying still, stiffly accepts the orange juice, and weakly, awkwardly, cautiously, pitifully begins to drink it. (The performer by this stage of the game knows that credibility of deliverance is essential.) The invisible nine-hundred-pound nurse, however, apparently satisfied that she has performed her duty, is evidently leaving, for another series of ponderously spaced, reverberating steps causes the orange juice to swill up and spill over. The patient, trying to wipe the stains off the hospital pajamas, is soon gasping and sputtering, drenched by a deluge of orange juice, and (at the hint of a giggle from the audience) begins frantically coughing, choking, flailing and kicking, then suddenly clutches into stiffness and falls off the couch with a painful-sounding thud onto the floor, dead, by the looks of it.

The observer, who is doubling over with irrepressible torrents of laughter, has lost! and has to run cross-legged to the bathroom, and then has to come up with another scene to challenge the other's ability to keep from laughing.

Another of our games was to stuff pillows up the fronts of our shirts and run around the living room like derailed bumper cars, head-on collisions being the preferred objective, as they caused us to ricochet backwards and land on the floor, stranded on our backs and giggling helplessly.

Harry, you missed out back then, you were stressed and lonely and driven in those years, and you didn't know what our generation has since learned, but I invite you, even though you're no longer with us in body, to go back there with me now, in case you're wondering if you should have been less harsh, and to receive my thanks, not only for the ways in which you provided for us, and for the ways in which you taught us, and for the love you felt but couldn't easily show back then, but even for that ceiling of imagined threat, beneath which Val and I discovered our future selves, our now present selves, people capable of levity despite the gravity.

There is nothing to judge, and therefore nothing to forgive. There is only observing, making friends with, and empowering all of the parts of ourselves with enormous appreciation for how creatively we have interacted after all.

6

Flying Fish

If we are, indeed, from some higher perspective, composing the elements of our lives, being the author of our own autobiographies, is it possible to discover a theme, a motif, an intended symphony of events that tells us we have been involved in a more masterful and well-designed creation than we knew? Can we become open not only to current synchronicities but to the overall interwoven pattern of this particular life-dream?

When I considered the possibility, I returned to my earliest memory as the potential first note or opening scene of my current lifetime. The question was, does a first memory stay vivid because of its isolated impact, or is its impact the result of its inherent importance in a life story?

That first memory, I discovered when I delved more deeply into it, was even more detailed than I'd expected.

I was two years old when my grandfather invited my 26-year-old mother and me to join him on a ferry boat ride to Catalina Island.

Going back, I can feel my short, then-blonde hair being blown straight back. My eyes are squinting into the wind as I watch the spinning diamonds sparkling on the dark choppy waves. I am sitting by the railing, on my mother's lap, on the skirt of her red and white polka-dotted dress with those padded shoulders in fashion in 1946, facing my grandfather. His thin hair is gray, and he is wearing a somewhat shiny dark gray suit. I can look up over my shoulder and see the glossy roll of dark brown hair atop my mother's forehead being relentlessly loosened into streaming strands, and her bright red lips and dark brown eyes laughing anyway. Warmed by the sun, listening to the roar of the engine over the slap of the waves and the occasional happy shouts of conversation, I grow drowsy. My eyelids grow heavy, and I slump back against my mother, and doze.

Suddenly I gasp, startled into jerking upright. I hold my breath, staring at the opalescent creature that has landed in my lap. It is as immobile as if it too is breathless and in awe as it gazes up at me, its long fins spread awkwardly across my outstretched legs. There are excited words exchanged between my mother and my grandfather as he reaches forward. Carefully grasping the fins between thumbs and forefingers, he fans out the silvery "wings", a shimmering, opalescent array of pinks and aqua greens.

My grandfather slipped the flying fish back into the sea, but my inner vision hovers within the sense of awe being exchanged between myself and a creature of breathless beauty, within the inhalation of impossibly beautiful hues shimmering across glistening wings. Folded into that memory is the sense of having been introduced to a world of miracles and blessings, angels and aliens, messages from ethereal otherworldly beings.

I was in my forties when I took another look at the map of my life and noticed that from my earliest childhood memory was a line connecting directly to another place and time indicated by the exact same symbol.

Seventeen years later I had seen the flying fish again, this time a school of them, for the second time in my life. I was nineteen, leaning on the railing of an ocean liner, cruising the Pacific along the California coast, embarking on a trip around the world. My mother had pulled me from my third semester at college to accompany her on her dream-of-a-lifetime come true. We were taking this trip because my grandfather had left her the money to do so when he died.

I looked from one point on the map to the other. Here we have little Lesta in a little ferry boat, crossing a little of the Pacific to an island, accompanied by her mother at the invitation of her grandfather. And over here we have bigger Lesta, about to cross the big Pacific on a big ocean liner, traveling with her mother because her grandfather had provided the means to do so. Now, let me get this right. Here we have little Lesta, being introduced to a world of blessings and surprises. And here we have bigger Lesta, being introduced to a much bigger world, not only of blessings and surprises, but of heavy-duty insights and gravity-dictated dichotomies. A single flying fish marks the first threshold, and a school of them the second. The grandfather at the first is gone by the second, but another male person walks into the vacancy at this very moment, stepping up to the railing behind nineteen-year-old Lesta and tickling her in the ribs. "Gotcha!"

"Oh! You startled me!"

"I've noticed you like coming out here by yourself. I was going to ask you to dance," twenty-five-year-old Parker says, leaning his arms on the railing beside her.

And thus started an innocent romance that eventually got lost in all the criss-crossings of the map, but forty-something me, now hot on the trail, traces another line to another point, another seventeen years later. Wow. This is the year Parker died. This is also the year I built my house and gave birth to my daughter (whose first initials are, coincidentally, FF, as in Flying Fish). This is the point at which I entered into yet another world. I thought it was the world of settling down and being devoted to family, but it was also the world of opening up to communications from the other side. It was at once a deeper delving into the material plane, becoming immersed in midlife responsibilities, and an inclusion of a greater reality in my perception, as I began to share with Parker not only the experience of his death, but what had happened immediately after, and what he had learned since.

I leaned back from the mental map I'd been reviewing and thought about the wavelengths in lifetimes that have specific frequencies. I knew about seven-year cycles. Now I'd discovered a seventeen-year cycle by connecting the dots between significant events in the expansion of my awareness. Was I onto something here? And if so, what?

But it was time to return a book I'd borrowed, even though I wasn't quite finished with it. Maybe I would read just a few more pages before I relinquished it. I flipped it open to one of the last chapters of the autobiography, and a pair of words jumped out at me, repeated several times in the first paragraph. Nikos Kazantzakis had paused, shaken, in front of a palace wall painting in Crete, on which was depicted a *flying fish* with outspread fins, leaping into the air. "I experienced great agitation and fellow feeling as I gazed at this flying fish, as though it was my own soul… the fish which leaps in order to transcend necessity and breathe freedom… to transcend destiny and unite with God."

Goosebumps! I *was* onto something! Wasn't it a fish that had made Jung notice synchronicity? My soul was dropping hints for me, leaving a trail through my life that I could map out!

By the time another seventeen years had passed, I casually remarked to a friend that I was on the verge of a major transition, about to enter the next realm in the expanding spheres of my consciousness. "How do you know?" Brad asked.

"I've noticed this pattern in my life. Every seventeen years I have a breakthrough experience. It takes me a couple of years to let the new reality sink in and take effect, and then I'm into it full swing, with a whole new take on everything."

Brad pulled out his books on astrology. "Wow. You're talking about the one-fifth cycles of Uranus. You *are* on the verge of a major transition! Right now! This month!" He ran his finger down the page. "Today!"

Oh, my, now we're getting complex! Is that what the planets do, weave spiraling wavelengths of information and transformation into our lives? Just how big *is* this pattern of interwoven influences?

My flying fish soul chuckles. It's *big*, baby. It's big.

7

Just a Reminder

As I mentioned in *Somewhere between Kindergarten and God*, a number of gifts were given to me by a family of light beings in a series of spontaneous visual meditations that started during my forty-fourth year. Over the course of a few months, I would occasionally find myself, just before falling asleep, in a round room with thirteen doors. During each visitation, one being of light would enter through one of the doors, join me at the oval table in the center of the room, and hand me an ethereal gift.

After considering all twelve of the gifts from various angles, I concluded that they were actually all the same gift -- the one I could carry with me through the thirteenth door, over the threshold between worlds -- as my reminder to others of all our many gifts.

If they *are* all the same gift, it occurred to me, I could ask myself, what is it? What's it called? I could consider them with this in mind, and find their common denominator.

Okay.

Is that okay?

Sure, go ahead.

Who, me? Oh, okay, so what were the twelve again?

The twelve of us, or the twelve gifts?

Whoa. The twelve of you? Someone's here from the twelve of you?

You seem to be forgetting something. Why don't we start with the twelve gifts, and take it from there?

Okay.

The first gift is *paradox*: the ability to broaden my perspective to encompass even what appear to be mutually exclusive truths within the one truth of Reality. Is God so omnipotent that S/H/We can create a perfectly unique individual who is exactly the same as everyone else? Yes, because in the bigger picture, all of creation consists of the same ethereal energy that subdivides itself into an infinite spectrum of differences without ever losing its original essence. I am unique and I am the same as everything else. *Either/or, neither/nor*, and *but* all become *and*. To substitute the word *and* for *but* is to allow my mind the expansiveness of its original nature. I could put my hand through this wall, but that's impossible. I could put my hand through this wall, and that's impossible. Oh. I could put my hand through this wall! *And* that's impossible! Both! I could heal myself from this disease instantly, but healing takes time. I could heal myself from this disease instantly, and healing takes time. *But* cancels half the truth. *And* revives a bigger truth from which to choose one's preference.

Paradox, the inclusion of all possibilities, shoves one philosophical interpretation of reality, that of logic, into a narrow stratum within an infinite spectrum. It unravels the hold that mind has on the world of separation and frees it to be inclusive of all possible and parallel and alternative and contradictory aspects of the One. Within the multiverse of infinite variety, all is not only possible, all possibilities exist at the same time. Can I unconditionally love myself, even when I'm being unloving? Can I embrace everything by letting everything go? Unconditional love, like a vast blanket of snow, includes the snowflake moments of being not only unloving, but also wrathful and despondent and bored out of my gourd. Embracing everything means I can even embrace not embracing everything, and letting go of everything means I can even let go of letting go. I can stop being afraid of my fear. I can stop judging myself for being judging. I can be at peace with not being at peace. I can intend and create my future by surrendering to whatever it will be. I can be in the dark and in the light at the same time. I can love everything that will unfold, even not loving what I'm experiencing, because I have been granted the paradox of myself, and the giver of the gift is always with me, for the giver of the gift is the very smallest part of me, and the vastest. If I can give myself such a gift, I can do anything. If I can do anything, can I create a living experience so big that I can never live it all?

Oh, how miraculously incomprehensible is the great Mystery, and how easily comprehended! The more I love the Mystery, the more it reveals Itself to me.

The second gift is *guidance*: the ability to draw to myself that which can be interpreted as communication with Spirit. Like a heart-shaped locket, this gift is even more comforting once the clasp is released. Open the heart, and I am reminded of how much I'm loved, and by whom. Someone or something that is me and not me wants me to find the secret, the hidden treasure, the genuine pleasure of being alive, and is leaving me clues, everywhere. Life is forever carrying on a conversation consisting of metaphors, and all I need is eyes to see, ears to hear, and a heart that feels the truth.

Culmination and source, the third gift, is the recognition of myself as the culmination of everything that has flowed into me, and as the source of everything that flows forth from me. I am, as is everyone, a unique vortex in the flow of time, transforming the vast past of genetics, personal and global history, familial and societal culture, soul lives and spirit that has been poured into me -- into an infinite influence that spreads outward, physically, emotionally, socially, economically, mentally, spiritually, and energetically, from my actions and my being.

The fourth gift is called *reflections of the One*. We are the mirrors, the images, the facets, the manifestations of universal consciousness discovering and creating itself. I'd forgotten this gift, this remembrance, so thoroughly by the time I was in my thirties that I had to look at myself in the mirror, several hours at a time, several times, while I talked and cried and laughed and scowled and beamed, until what I was looking at was no longer subject to my critical eye, my scorn or anxiety, until I was so disassociated from the image and meaning of "me" by over-exposure that I could finally simply see someone whose emotions touched me and whose ugliness didn't override her beauty. Because I'd finally seen myself as other than some embarrassing mistake, I no longer despaired or feared that others could see me. I was eager to see them. And I did. I saw others whose emotions touched me and whose ugliness and beauty were the same. The more I looked into the mirror, the more I could see, mirrored in everything around me, the perfection within the imperfection, the essence within the differences, the lovable within the disturbing, the wisdom behind the ignorance. It's all the same Amazing Face.

Peace is the gift of gentling my experience with love and trust and the serene confidence that all is exactly as it needs to be. So I can just relax, immerse myself in ease and rest assured: what needs to be taken care of is being taken care of, and what needs to happen is happening. I can radiate peace into any situation simply by trusting its value and necessity in the greater picture.

An *intelligent aura*, the sixth gift, naturally and fluidly draws in what is healthy and growth-enhancing, repels what isn't, and emits what is beneficial to those around me. When I am in need of something, I will attract what I need. When I need nothing, nothing will invade me. When I have something to give, whoever needs to receive it will appear. The instincts, intuitions, and signals of my ethereal self are acutely accurate and reliable. I need only adjust the gauges of this wetsuit body to align with what my sixth-through-seventieth senses are revealing, and I will be as fluid as the sea of light around me.

Self-evident purpose frees me from trying to determine what my purpose is in any given moment, as my every act is preparation, elucidation, enactment, or fulfillment of my reason for being, as is that of a child or the wind or a tree. Self-evident purpose includes the natural propensity to change as well as the natural willingness to accept what is. There is no need to determine the difference, only to be whatever my differences are.

Through the eighth gift, *astral travel*, I can put my body on hold while I visit with those who need love and healing, or connect with the network of loving beings surrounding the planet, or re-enter the Source for my own replenishment. I can slip out of my body as a single point of consciousness and perceive what my normal senses cannot. If I were more advanced in the use of this gift, I could slip out of my body as a double of myself and affect what is beyond my physical reach. I can release my perception spherically. By experiencing my every heartbeat as a spherical wave, one pulsing bubble of energy flowing outward, followed by another and another, I can catch one of the beats, ride the bubblewave, and be borne instantaneously into the immensity of love, where the galaxies are deep within me and I am All That Is.

Memory of past and future helps me to put this moment, this tiny lifetime, into perspective. In this moment, all possible pasts and all possible futures are available to me if I need to draw on them. The more I remember that there are any number of pasts and futures, the more I can create who I want to be, now. The more I treasure what I've known and will know, the more I can appreciate this moment's uniqueness.

Lucid dreaming reminds me that I am merely one character in my soul's dream. Whether this dream is a nightmare or a sweet dream, I know that I will understand it when I awake. I can begin to understand it even while I'm dreaming. I can learn to determine the outcome of my dream. As an aspect of the One who dreams, I am contributing to the ever-evolving consciousness of the original lucid Dreamer.

The eleventh gift, that of *happiness*, is the gift of joyful appreciation for the forgetfulness in which I chose to wrap my present so I could delight in the unraveling of its mystery. It is gratitude for the wonders and miracles of life, for they are everywhere.

When there seemed to be no more gifts forthcoming from the Beings of Light, my then-eight-year-old daughter gave me the twelfth, which she called the *fountain of youth*: I can be, in any given moment, any age I want to be. I can be an infant, an adolescent, a hundred-thousand-year-old soul, or the infinite Being itself. I can walk out of my role of maturity, stoop into the curiosity of a three-year-old before an anthill, straighten up into the tired longing-to-go-home of a ninety-year-old, turn on the car radio and show them how to dance behind the wheel, and snuggle into bed as if it were a womb, all in a single hour. Or I can pretend that I am just one age for an entire year.

That's it, all twelve gifts. Are you still here, the twelve of you?

There are more than twelve of us, and you are one of us.

Yes, I am, I am a light being. So is my daughter, and so are many people, maybe even all people, whether or not they remember that. Are all people light beings?

Oh, the possibilities of how we've all divided are absolutely infinite.

Will you tell me more?

Any time.

Okay, then I'll get back to you.

Yes, you will, and you'll catch up to us as well.

Sounds like a merry-go-round.

As merry as you'd like it.

Well, I think I'm going to have to get serious, occasionally. I mean, this is serious business, living on this planet, in its present condition.

As you will. You have the freedom to experience it however you desire.

Freedom. That's one of the common denominators of the gifts, isn't it?

8

Take a Yellow Bus

I can see that the common denominator of the twelve gifts might be called a lot of things: consciousness, universal truth, love, the power of transformation, divine wisdom, and, yes, most definitely, freedom. Every one of the twelve gifts can be seen as an aspect of freedom. The first one that jumps out at me is the memory of past and future.

Being able to remember the past and the future is freedom? As in freedom from pain, freedom to let go, freedom to act, freedom to love life?

I am being informed that this is so.

Take a yellow school bus, for example; take a yellow school bus and place it into the context of several different times, and it becomes an instrument of freedom.

To a nine-year-old boy in nineteenth-century Ireland, who goes with his Da to the coal mines every day, day after day, from before sunrise to after dark, who comes home weary and smudged to potatoes for dinner, crawls in under a meager blanket as close to the hearth as he can, and listens to his father coughing all night, a peek into the future would make a yellow school bus look like a glowing royal carriage. Are ye tellin' me it goes 'round the entire county and picks up every single one of the children, and they don't have to pay? They go to a buildin' where they get fed? They get to learn to read? But what about me Da, who'd be helpin' him at the mines? He and me mother could both work someplace else and come home in the daylight? I wouldn't have to work until I was ready to *choose* what I wanted to do? Ooh, I'd be sayin' now there's a change for the better! How long d'ya say we'll be waitin' fer this most amazin' vehicle to be makin' its appearance, then?

To a nine-year-old girl in twenty-second-century South Africa, who is opting between apprenticing with a woman who gives tours to the sacred sites on Mars and a man who transcribes conversations with dolphins onto crystal discs, to this girl who rides the free Transatlantic tube by herself in a totally safe world to have lunch with her favorite aunt in Venezuela and to spend the night at her father's resort on Antarctica's balmy coast, a yellow school bus would seem like a prison wagon on its way to the Inquisition. You mean it ran on a fuel that poured poison into the air? And it collected all the people who weren't yet seventeen? They were compelled under penalty of law (what's that?) to stay in one building all day, every day, and eat reconstituted potatoes? They were forced to learn what they had no interest in? They were numbed into denying their true adventure? How could their families watch them climb aboard a yellow bus without crying?

To a nine-year-old boy in animal skins, stalking a rabbit with his spear to bring back to the cave, a yellow bus filled with shouting children in pink and purple nylon jackets would be a staggering sight, a futuristic phenomenon beyond his comprehension. Its cultural significance might also be lost, among the myriad artifacts of ancient primitive cultures, on a nine-year-old girl stopping into Earth-uv-Sol's twenty-first century on her way to flitting among the Incas before visiting the seventh moon of Zeah-uv-Arn.

To put a yellow school bus, or any cultural symbol, into the perspective gained from memory of past and future, is to claim the freedom of detached involvement. Attributing whatever historical significance we choose to a yellow school bus – regarding one century's solution to a problem as the next century's problem in need of a solution, or one century's mode of transportation or education as merely a step between the previous and ensuing modes – frees us to appreciate the transitory nature of our present cultural givens. Appreciating the transitory nature of anything gives us an insight into our choices regarding it. We can ignore it, shrug it out of our reality; we can maintain it as an acceptable facet of our reality; we can improve upon it, change it to fit into the ideal reality we want to create; or we can simply observe it, keep it in perspective. We can be detached and/or involved. And when we're free to identify with it however we will, we are also freed from judging another's identification with it.

I was called into the high school principal's office, to meet with him, the vice-principal, and a teacher, because my son had been caught making wooden bowls in Industrial Arts class (or shop, as it was called in my day). Not salad bowls. Bowls for smoking weed. Marijuana pipes. Oh. Well. Whew. How many bowls did he make before he was caught?

Fourteen.

My hand flew up to cover my mouth. I studied the carpet with a frown so they wouldn't notice my irrepressible smile. Eric got away with making fourteen bowls before he was caught?

Of course I didn't tell the principal, the vice-principal, and the shop teacher that I was tickled by my son's cleverness, or that the shop teacher's supervision seemed to be more the issue here. I understood their position and didn't want to force them into defending it. They wouldn't be participating in an institution of education if they didn't believe in its inherent value, would they? At the least they wouldn't want to be told they were missing the point, when they were putting hours of their weeks, years of their lives, into something that, hopefully, they believed in. And that they were worried about the connection of the bowls to their function was also understandable, within their cultural givens. So I told them that since Eric had experimented with pot and had discarded it as much less exciting than his own mental clarity, and since I had all the same wood-working equipment at home in my own shop, which he was welcome to use, it seemed to me that my son's sole reason for making fourteen bowls in class was a sixteen-year-old boy's eagerness to impress his friends with how much he could get away with. This didn't put the teacher into the best light. So I hurried to add that although I was not concerned about my son's habits or intentions, I agreed that his behavior could be considered unacceptable within the environment of mutually respected boundaries they were trying to uphold. I hoped I was helping them take the least oppressive action. Apparently I'd found a non-fear-based resonance – drug use was a no-no, vociferous rebellion was not to be tolerated, but these men could relate to a teenage boy showing off to his peers, and the decided-upon punishment (for the crime of audacity) was a compromise Eric and I could live with, in view of where the institution of education lies on a historical scale.

It's not always easy to remember to take advantage of all the opportunities we're presented with to exercise our freedom. I regretted a later incident, when my daughter Fawni was shamed by another principal's invasion of her privacy, a letter of hers having been found in her friend's locker and handed to me to read. When I robotically accepted and read the letter, I wasn't being mindful of *her* right not to be judged out of context – for her own experimentation with reality, which she had described in detail to a friend. She and I both suffered the consequences of an unfair and resented punishment. But that experience did remind me to notice when my freedom of perspective is inoperative. It's inoperative when I'm stressing myself out by swearing at the guy who just cut me off in traffic. I'm not exercising my freedom of detached involvement in any situation where my anger can't flow into disinterest, acceptance, insight, or improvement.

Fawni (nearing twenty at the time this was written) came into my upstairs home office, leaned on my shoulders, and read the previous paragraph. "Wow, Mom, it's so weird that you were writing about that time in high school! I just finished writing a letter to that principal!"

"Really?" (I love when that happens.)

"Yeah. I don't need to send it or anything, I just wanted to tell him, for my own sake, how he could have handled that situation. Wanna read it?"

"Sure." And I am, because I have just been considering this, impressed by how my daughter has spontaneously improved upon the past for herself, with her hindsight, as she addresses a self-elected patriarchal power-tripper and tells him exactly how that moment could and should have been handled, with consciousness and sensitivity. She has made it even clearer to me that while the present includes the specific past that created it, it also includes any number of ways to relive the past, and thereby to recreate the future. To know this is to bring the present self into its most empowering freedom. I watch my daughter walk into her future without leaving that part of her past self forgotten in a corner, and I see a young woman who has presence.

We can time travel, right from our own living rooms. We can change the past, and therefore the present, and with it, the future. The memory of all pasts and all futures, or at least the awareness that there really are an unlimited number of them, gives us such poetic license to write and rewrite this story we call life.

9

The Word

There was a powerful urgency, at certain times in history, as well as a powerful resistance, to the spreading of the Word. Because the Word had lost something in the translation, not only for the converts but, unbeknownst to them, for the missionaries as well, a conflict of interests arose. Apparently the conflict is being resolved. It seems it has become impossibly easy to spread the Word. In fact, it has become impossible *not* to spread the Word.

When my friend Dick read the original Lord's Prayer (translated directly from the Aramaic into English rather than through Greek and Latin) to our discussion group, I asked him where he'd gotten it and with whom I could check for permission to pass it on. He'd received it over the Internet and didn't know where it had originated, but he assumed, from its contents, that were I to continue to pass it along, the translator would not be unhappy about more people getting the message. I emailed it to several friends. A month later it came back to me from the other side of the country from someone whose connection I couldn't trace. But then, it had already been making the rounds before I got it. I expect it's been around the globe a number of times by now. If I am out of line repeating it here, I hope someone will let me know what I can do to correct the situation, besides thanking them for having corrected the situation. Making the Word so easy to hear by bringing it closer to home is doing us all a favor. As our friend Brooke put it, with tears in her eyes, when Dick had finished reading the prayer: "Oh, my, can you imagine what your life would be like, what the world would be like, if *this* had been the prayer you said in school every day?"

Can you imagine, if this had been what was shared between the itinerant white culture and the indigenous peoples, how differently they would have regarded one another?

Better yet, can you imagine what is happening to humanity now that we *are* exchanging this prayer and so many other open-hearted words all around the world?

O cosmic Birther of all radiance and vibration! Soften the ground of our being and carve out a space within us where Your Presence can abide. Fill us with Your creativity so that we may be empowered to bear the fruit of Your mission. Let each of our actions bear fruit in accordance with our desire. Endow us with the wisdom to produce and share what each being needs to grow and flourish. Untie the tangled threads of destiny that bind us, as we release others from the entanglement of past mistakes. Do not let us be seduced by that which would divert us from our true purpose, but illuminate the opportunities of the present moment. For You are the ground and the fruitful vision, the birth-power and the fulfillment, as all is gathered and made whole once again.

It's comforting to hear the original intent of that prayer.

I especially like the phrasing of that last line, for it seems that in many areas, all is indeed being gathered and made whole once again.

One of the schisms that is currently being bridged into a continuum is the one between science and religion, or, more specifically, between physics and metaphysics, and, apparently, between biology and what I'm tempted to call metabiology. Recently advanced theories about a connection between DNA and quantum evolution have catapulted scientists into a multiverse of infinite potential, but before I offer you what I've gleaned from those theories, let me take you on a little trip into the Void.

If you don't care to join me – if you're not as fond of leaping into the unknown as I am – please feel free to skip this part! See you in the next chapter.

If you do care to wander into weird time and deep space with me, I'll start with the concept that triggered my plunge.

Deepak Chopra, who is adept at interweaving physics and metaphysics in his discussions of quantum healing, has proposed that the capacity of our minds to interpret and create our realities is not a product of our physical bodies or brains. He suggests that it is the other way around. Our bodies are the products, the manifestations, of our minds, and our brains are simply the relay between a greater Mind at large and our own individual minds. We are not mind within body, but body within Mind. Non-local, decentralized, universal Mind supplies us with an infinite amount of information. (We are constantly being in-*form*ed. These bodies that we assume to be solid and substantial are in fact flowing and ephemeral. We have entirely different bodies, containing entirely different atoms, within a relatively short period of time.) Since we are imbued with Mind, are part of this Intelligence, we are capable of editing the information. We are constantly recreating ourselves from a field of information. Our thoughts choose what information to supply to our bodies and our bodies comply as manifestations of our interpretations.

Upon hearing this, I felt challenged to understand the connection between universal information and our thoughts. What is this universal information, physically speaking? What is it we are translating into thoughts, words, instruments of creative action? Where is it located? In the atoms? How do atoms whizzing into and out of our bodies supply us with intelligence?

Atoms, comparable perhaps to miniature solar systems, consist of little spheres of energy. But what is energy? It's motion. The protons, the electrons, all those subatomic whirligigs, are, in my mind's eye, little time-loaded bubbles of motion in a sea of tranquility -- they spin, vibrate, zoom along, undulate, or otherwise perform acts of movement, within a vast something/nothing that appears to move at a different rate, or no rate at all. They are packets of pure change, or pockets of time, tiny events happening at a frequency different from that of whatever is around them.

And what is it they are moving in, moving through?

When we give it a name, like space or ether or consciousness or unified field or quantum foam or cosmic birther or God, we are simply trying to understand that an eternal, infinite something/nothing is subdividing itself into different finite, measurable frequencies, and that this motion, this energy, in contrast to stillness, is the something/nothing defining itself as something happening here and nothing happening there. Here it's in motion, there it isn't. Here it's on, there it's off.

On, off. On, off. This is the basic modus operandi of a binary language. The binary basis of information-relay used by computers is doing its thing way out there in the cosmos and way deep down in here, inside of us. On, off, dit, dah, dit, dit, dah, the message is coming through, an immeasurable amount of information flowing through everything that exists of subatomic particles, which is everything that exists, as far as we can tell, in this particular set of dimensions, anyway, whether or not we consider it to be alive. We are constantly being bombarded, we are part of, we are made up of, zillions of tiny time-traveling bits of information in a vast arena of Now.

So how do we know what the information is? How do we interpret it and make use of it?

Although there may be a few gaps across which must be made synapses of faith, I think the answer is beginning to bridge itself between the physical and the metaphysical realms with the latest theory in the field of quantum mechanics, that of quantum evolution.

Quantum mechanics is the name given to the discovery that everything that *can* happen, on a subatomic level, *does* happen. A subatomic particle can exist in two places at once. It can exist in a trillion places at once. It can do whatever the observer wants it to do. Or not. It can travel backwards and sideways in time. It can affect another particle that has no evident connection to it. It can behave like a wave.

The reason fundamental particles can be in many places, many states, and many times all at once, some quantum physicists are theorizing, is that they actually exist not just in the universe we are capable of perceiving, but in all the possible and probable, parallel and alternate realities of the entire multiverse.

This theory was arrived at in answer to a question posed by biologist Johnjoe McFadden in his book *Quantum Evolution*. Mutations have been assumed, until recently, to be random trial-and-error promotions of the survival of a species when the species can no longer use what it has to get what it needs. But, McFadden asks, what if mutations are not random? What if evolution is occurring at the quantum level – by design?

It isn't just subatomic particles that appear to be behaving multi-dimensionally. Molecules have been witnessed to do so as well. Which leads these scientists into expecting that even more complex systems are also multi-dimensional. They aren't yet considering the complex systems known as human beings, but they are contemplating the likelihood of DNA molecules doing what the subatomic particles of DNA already appear to be doing -- dashing in and out of the parallel realities of the multiverse. Which startles them into this whole new take on biological evolution. What if the DNA of a species can check out all the alternatives in the quantum multiverse, and then, having selected a particular one, introduce into its life form the best possible change for the best possible results?

Although there are many interpretations of what has been observed in the quantum realm, it is generally agreed upon by physicists that something enters the quantum state when it is isolated from its three-dimensional environment – *something enters the multi-dimensional state when it is isolated* -- and returns when there is once again a sufficient energy exchange with its physical environment. A cell that experiences survival-threatening isolation from its environment can slip into the multiverse, scan the infinite available possibilities, equip itself with what it needs to reconnect, and slip back into this universe to keep on growing and multiplying. This process has been demonstrated in the lab with bacteria cells.

What we're talking about here, on a subatomic level, a cellular one, and, for that matter, a human one, is the infinite freedom of creative choice.

Something enters the multi-dimensional state when it is isolated. The isolation from an energy-exchanging environment that serves as the propellant into the multiverse of all realities can, as I see it, be experienced in any number of ways by us humans. It can result from a near-fatal accident, a terminal disease, a hallucinogenic drug, an isolation tank, solitary confinement, meditation, an out-of body experience, the presence of an angel dissolving the veil, the sudden rush of euphoria within a state of grace.

These states are plunges into the Void, into that sea of tranquility within which those time-bubbles are doing their dance, into that information-rich vastness which Chopra calls universal Mind, and which McFadden calls the multiverse.

We can choose the method of separating from three-dimensional reality, and we can choose from the multiverse what we want to bring back with us, be it miracle or madness, strength or surrender, gradual development or instantaneous enlightenment.

How can we learn to do this? How can we learn to choose what information to substantiate into our bodies and our experiences?

We don't have to learn how to! We are already, unconsciously, translating the information -- into part of another letter O or Omega in yet another reference book on the amazing feats and hands of the almighty multiverse. We've been doing so for eons.

One of the most awesome discoveries reported about our chromosomes by Matt Ridley in his book *Genome* is that they are the biological Akashic records of our entire evolution, from the first single living cell, all the way through the changes of the eons, to these billions of multi-trillion-cell human bodies. The unbroken chain of information we've inherited from that first cell still includes every chapter, every page, every word of every subsequent expansion on the theme, of our entire journey as organic entities.

This information is replicated, passed on, maintained, and added to in a quadrinary language. (I don't know if quadrinary is a word. I'm guessing that since a binary language consists of two components, quadrinary would describe a language of four alphabetical bits of information.) The language isn't spoken, as far as we know, although I imagine it might emit sounds, since it is made of moving parts, vibrating elements. Neither is it written, not in symbols that we would call letters, although scientists have tagged letters to the four elements that copy and translate information into our cells from previous cells, so that they (the scientists) can read the series of three-letter-amino-acid-words strung around the double helix of a DNA molecule.

Our genes are literally like groups of words, paragraphs similar to recipes. The chemicals that make up our genes are like words, and the elements that make up those chemicals are like letters of the alphabet. If you build a word from a few hydrocarbon molecules, and add a few adjectives, you can "read" the result as organic life. Attach a few more modifiers and you are reading organic plant life, or a few more and you read organic animal life. Add to that a few hundred thousand chemical and genetic modifiers, and you're reading a human being.

We humans are "read-outs" of these zillions of bits of information. Each of us is a living character in an incomprehensibly complex plot.

Does a character in a story have choices? Is it a story, this evolution of our human race from a single cell into these present billions of separate individuals? If we agree that it is a story, does it have an Author? Or are we authoring it ourselves?

A character in a story is sometimes a familiar aspect of the author, and sometimes a surprising stranger, a creation that creates itself as it is being created. Each character, as a facet of the author, is imbued not only with the entire plot up to this point, but with all the drafts that went into the wastebasket. Each character, as a separate spontaneously self-creative function, is adding his or her own twist to the outcome.

We have taken on lives of our own, reflecting back to the Author more of who and what this agent of change is, this stupendous phenomenon, this self-aware cosmic intelligence. We've been faxed from the original office, added our own memos, and are faxing ourselves back by the nano-second.

We are the Word made flesh, the Logos incarnate, the living story of the forever-changing-and-unchanging All.

We don't have to learn how to translate the information or how to choose what we do with it. We need only recognize that we are already doing so, and then do so consciously, by watching our translations: our thoughts. There is no central intelligence agency dictating precise outcomes. The outcomes, like the zillions of bits of information themselves, are always in flux. This is the way in which apparently impossible miracles can happen. This is the beauty of the mystery.

Both Ridley and Chopra, coming at this concept of decentralized authority or authorship from different directions, and witnessing it on different levels, offer a similar opinion on its character. Ridley is led to conclude that the human genome, operating in different ways from different cells, maintains a mystique, a bit of the trickster in its fashioning of behavior. It's somewhat unpredictable. It seems to have an attitude. Chopra describes the Indian term Maya, the mask of the mysterious force behind it all, as not just illusion, but camouflage, paradox, magic, deception, a trickster. Maya is the script, the costumes, the roles, the stage scenery, and it can be all-powerful, totally absorbing and convincing, or it can be utterly impotent, depending on one's perspective. When you strip away the levels of Maya, when you probe this apparently solid body, descend through the unfolding story being written by the genome, and pass through the quantum particles that are darting in and out of the multiverse, you arrive at nothing, and it is this nothing from which we generate ourselves. Our original nature is nothing if it is not playful. The Word is Play?!

Let us flourish, let us create, let us illuminate the opportunities of the present moment, as all is made whole once again.

10

Leave It to Them

Across the aisle from me, illuminated by the moonlight, was a picture I couldn't have captured with a camera. An Amazon-built, dark-skinned woman, with hundreds of beaded braids and an Egyptian profile, leaned back in the aisle seat, her eyes peacefully closed. One of her bejeweled hands rested gently on the tightly curled head in her lap, that of her petite husband, who was lying on his back with his knees pressed up against the window. Sprawled across his chest was their sleeping toddler, her bushy little head tenderly cupped by her mother's other hand. Shadows and silvery light flashed across their forms as the Greyhound cruised across another Midwestern state.

Everyone was finally getting some sleep. Even the gang in the back was quiet. I was the privileged one, witnessing this loveliness that I would have missed if I'd flown back to the East Coast from my visits to various family members in Oregon and Montana.

Several decades ago, taking a cross-country bus ride home from college was all about strangers remaining politely isolated from one another during a long quiet trip. I'd settled into the empty front seat on this trip and sensed immediately that I was about to find out how much leaving the driving to them has changed since then. Several voices in the back were raised in laughter and talk, some of it rather boisterous. The voices, one male voice in particular, had a bounce and a swagger, you know what I'm sayin'? Ha ha ha! All riiiight! Now you *talkin'*! You say what? Ha ha ha! I would soon discover that almost everyone aboard was either Afro-American or didn't speak English as their first language, if they spoke it at all.

I would also discover that after a couple of nights of being awakened every two hours, for a five-minute stop or a half-hour one, people from Portland, Seattle, Spokane, and points east would all become one big family, looking out for one another, making sure everyone was back on board, mumbling through their toothpaste in the restrooms and giving up on looking groomed. When you walk into a public restaurant with your matted hair sticking straight out from the back of your head and your clothes looking like they got pulled from the bottom of the dirty laundry basket, well, if you were the only one, you'd tend to sidle along the wall toward the restroom looking down at the floor so as to become invisible, but when there are thirty-seven of you, you're a tribe of sorts. Of all sorts. The folks in the back, having started out as strangers, crowded together for group photos in barren bus stops, blacks holding whites' kids in their arms and vice versa, arms across shoulders all the way around the semicircle, laughing and talking as their instamatics were handed to the front.

In some small town somewhere in the middle of the country, a lone teenager climbed aboard. He flung his backpack down on the seat behind me and immersed himself into the privacy of his Walkman. Two hours later, everyone, or almost everyone, piled out for lunch, leaving their bags on their seats. A sheriff, who had evidently been waiting for the bus, spoke to the bus driver, climbed aboard, and stood by the one remaining passenger, the teenaged white boy, during the entire stop.

Several travelers clustered around outside the bus after eating.

"I heared his parents phoned from de town vere he got on," an older Swedish woman shared. "Dey varned de sheriff dat deir son vas a t'ief."

Oh, my, I thought, how awful. What kind of *parents* would alert the cops to their son being a thief? I felt bad for the boy, glancing at him as I took my seat in front of him. He must be feeling so humiliated, so alienated. But what could anyone say?

One of the men, whom by now I recognized as the loudest of the laughers in the back, bounced up the stairs. "Where's that bad kid at?" Mildly shocked by his forwardness, I glanced up at him. "There he is." He paused in the aisle. I braced myself for what I expected him to say as he caught the boy's eye. "Mm, mm. Bad *family*. You hang in there, you hear?" He waited for the boy to acknowledge him. "You need something, you *talk* to us!" He lifted an eyebrow. "We here for you, man." His words, a heart-warming surprise, were followed by assents and nods from those who boarded after him.

The driver pulled into a parking lot as the sun was setting. "We'll be here for half an hour, folks. There's a mini-mart and a fast burger place to the left, and a fried chicken place to the right. Thirty minutes. Anyone who wants to stay on the bus is welcome to do so. Anyone who wants to stretch their legs, now's the time." He glanced at the teenager as he spoke, then opened the door and headed for the burger place. People shuffled forward, stretching. Everyone disembarked, leaving their belongings on their seats. I turned around and noticed that the last person out of the bus was the teenager. He didn't want to make eye contact with anyone, so no one bothered him. But twenty minutes later he was standing near the men who were having a cigarette before they got back on the bus.

I was so uplifted by the update on ground-level America that I almost didn't want to get off the bus. I wanted to keep traveling around the country, watching parents spread their coats out on the floor of another bus station for their sleepy children and rest their heads on one another's shoulders, listening to strangers laughing quietly as they shared their stories over cigarettes outside another convenience store, breaking the language barrier with some sweet old couple on their way to visiting their grandchildren, recording with my artist's eye moments of beauty in the moonlight.

So, later in the year, I took the bus again. The descending sun cast a rosy hue across the peaks of the lacy-white Rockies as the bus stopped on the outskirts of a small mountain town. We'd been flagged down by two hunters in orange vests standing beside their pickup truck. A thirteen-year-old boy climbed aboard. One of the hunters told the driver that the boy's mother would be waiting for him in Denver. The boy, who looked part Native American, passed between me and a carnival worker from Alabama, a woman who had unsuccessfully tried to engage the other passengers in a snowball fight at our last stop. The boy plumped himself into the empty seat behind her. I felt sorry for him, having to go home to his mom and school, no doubt, when he'd probably rather have stayed with his dad. I hoped the five-hour trip ahead of him wasn't all going to be spent wiping his cheeks with the back of his sleeve and staring out the window.

A few minutes later, at the regular bus stop in town, another hunter waved as his sandy-haired thirteen-year-old got on the bus and swung into the empty seat behind me.

The bus lumbered out of town. The first boy turned from the window and looked across the aisle. "You been huntin'?" he ventured.

"Yeah, and I got me a buck!"

"Yeah? Me, too. Four points. What was yours?"

"Four points. This your first?"

"Yeah."

"Mine, too. You goin' to Denver?"

"Yeah. You?"

"Yeah. What school you go to?"

After half an hour the conversation had picked up a rhythm.

"My dad went and shot a deer, and then he went and drank a beer..."

"And got himself poked up the rear..."

"And I said that was mighty queer..."

The carny and I rolled our eyes at each other. She turned around. "I bet you boys woulda had a snowball fight with me."

"Sure I woulda! I love snowball fights!"

"My dog can catch snowballs in his teeth! One time..."

And the stories began to roll. But they kept coming back to getting that first buck. Together the boys reveled in having crossed that threshold into manhood – "What kinda rifle you use?" -- until they fell asleep, across the aisle from one another, exhausted and content, half an hour before the bus pulled into Denver.

I found myself wondering if someone's guardian angel had had anything to do with this propitious meeting.

The woman from Alabama continued to comment on the beauty of the moonlit snow, a rare treat for her. She leaned across the aisle and told me about a mishap that she'd survived the last time she encountered snow.

"You must have a guardian angel," I finally had to venture, not really sure about how such an observation would be received.

"Oh, I do!" she exclaimed, as if the subject were brought up way too infrequently. "I do have a guardian angel! He's my half-brother. He died, but I jes' know it's him watchin' over me. Why, when I was sittin' in the passenger seat of my friend's car and he had to slam on the brakes, I hit the windshield so hard it shattered into a million pieces. Glass all over everything! But I didn't get a cut or a scratch on me, not a one! My guardian angel was between me and that windshield. And another time, when I was comin' home from work on my bike one night? This big ole truck comes thunderin' 'round the corner, goin' like the dickens. By his headlights I seen I was right in the middle of his lane, and I didn't have time to do nothin' about it, but my guardian angel got me outta that fix by this much." She held her thumb and finger a half inch apart. "This much, I swear."

As we stood in line at the Denver depot, shuffling our bags forward toward door number three, a newcomer worried out loud about the icy weather.

"I don't think we have anything to worry about," I offered, turning around. "This lady has a guardian angel."

She took the cue and reassured them with her stories. To my surprise, a few other people in line, even an unlikely-looking man in a black leather coat, began nodding and mentioning their guardian angels. They had been given permission to share their secret sense of being watched over. I was once again being given a whole new take on the many colors and shapes of guardian angels.

Before I'd boarded the bus at the start of this return trip across the country, I'd pulled a reading from a deck of Angel Cards. The Archangel Michael, I had read, will give you courage during trying times. My interest having been piqued, I'd decided to find out more about the Archangel Michael as soon as I got home. Watching Kansas roll by, I finally opened the book I'd brought along, a comprehensive and elucidating treatise on Rudolf Steiner's anthroposophy entitled *The Imagination of Pentecost,* by Richard Leviton, and I discovered, to my delight, that it happened to include a chapter devoted entirely to the Archangel Michael. With growing exhilaration I read that the Michael mission, now underway, is dedicated to igniting the Christ Consciousness in every single individual as a self-sovereign, self-aware facet of the Source. It is within each of us that the Second Coming is occurring. We are the voices of vision. We are the conscious forces of God toward truth and freedom. Michael is the spirit of the times, the birthing impulse within each of us, the courageous, loving urge to open to our divine nature, to move from abstract thinking into the warm, living awareness of spiritual resurrection in our lives.

The Michael message, in case I hadn't caught its personal significance, was given an unexpected signature. I stopped in Kansas City to visit friends who'd recently moved there, and as I stepped refreshed from a steaming shower, I glanced at the fogged-up mirror and did a double take. A word must have been written in lipstick by one of the previous household members and then wiped clean, but not so thoroughly that it didn't show up as a ghost of a name across the fogged glass. The name was Michael.

By the time I got home, I felt surrounded by angels. The kind who can reassure a lonely boy that someone recognizes him. The kind with whom we can relax, when we don't know where we're going, and leave the driving to them.

11

Tuning Forks

Does it really matter which path we take after all?

My sister spent over thirteen years living in a cult community. In exchange for a large, close-knit, loving, critical, submissive, co-dependent family and the dangled-carrot promise of Transformation with a capital T, she largely surrendered her individual right to determine how and where she could live, what and how much she could eat, and when and with whom she could sleep.

She still doesn't interpret her experience as having been that of an innocent victim, manipulated away from her true nature by someone who used his charisma to fulfill the unmet needs of his own distorted ego.

She sees it in its entirety as the means by which she uncovered, nurtured, tested, and finally merged with her true nature. At which point she left the community, and finally achieved the Transformation she'd been seeking.

She'd had no idea, having been denied access to TV, radio, magazines, newspapers, to any media at all, how much the world had blossomed from 1982 to 1996. She kept calling me, from all the places she was checking out as possibilities for starting fresh, exclaiming, "Lesta, the world is so wonderful! People are so great! Everyone I meet is so conscious and loving and present!"

She decided she wanted to find a home with a garden, get a "normal" job, have great women friends and a good man and two cats in her life, and raise chickens. Within a year and a half she'd established herself in

Montana, with all of the above. Her transformation from self-critical migraine-suffering subject to confident, openhearted self-sovereign woman was complete, and utterly astounding.

Is it possible that no matter what she went through, she would have found herself not broken but strengthened, triumphantly in love with life after all and eager to experience more of her own choices? Did she come into this life planning to be prepared by the loneliness and independence of her younger years to win certain endurance tests? Might she have been just as motivated to summon her physical stamina, her emotional resilience, and her spiritual awakening by a couple of bad marriages? a few years in a concentration camp? a treacherous accident? Could that somewhat misunderstood, uncertain little girl have become this actively involved, generously out-going woman by the time she reached her forties without those *particular* years of frustration, delusion, and despair countered by joy, love, and learning? Is it possible that her original nature, the essence with which she was born, although it was withdrawn from interactions at a young age, would gradually have emerged again simply with the passage of time through the spectrum of human experience?

Maybe what I'm asking here is, how much does it matter which direction we choose when we come to those forks in the road? I mean, does *everything* happen for a reason? Is it *all* meant to be? Must we *always* look back and say, oh, wow, I couldn't have gotten here without having experienced that. Maybe we *could* have gotten here without having experienced that. Don't we have an original nature that will shine through sooner or later, no matter what we do?

Ah, you have finally posed the question so that it contains its own answer. Yes, you do have an original nature, and it is so vast and complex and so pure and simple that it is in every experience, it exists underneath and around and in between everything, and so it only matters what you choose if it matters to who you are in the form you are creating at this time. Whether or not you loll around and do nothing, or let everything be done to and for you, or actively participate in doing something, and whether or not that something seems good or bad, catalytic or deadening, it is all part of the Great Experience.

Okay, you're getting a little too far ahead of me here. Let me back up a little. So I took a certain path, I did this, didn't do that, got here, and here I am, and so, does it *matter* which way I go now? How do

I see past the expectations created by fears and fairy tales? I mean, okay, sometimes it becomes just so obvious, the pain far outweighs the pleasure as soon as you take a mincing baby step in that direction, so you pull your foot back and head right, or the guilt is enough to turn you away from the deed before it's done, or the way in which you'll help someone else is so worth it compared to getting a little something for yourself. Those are, relatively speaking, easy decisions – although, personally, I've never found decisions to be easy. So why am I so hooked on choices anyway? Choices are not always fun. Like those times when you just can't see how one set of good-plus-not-so-good outweighs the other set of good-plus-not-so-good, but there it is, the fork in the road. You can't just sit there and wait for the fork to disappear.

Actually, if you back up a little more, you can see how that might happen.

What, the fork could disappear?

Well, so to speak. Would there appear to be a fork there if you were satisfied with what you have?

Oh, I see where you're going. No, no, I'm not talking about becoming dissatisfied.

Oh, okay, because if you were, you could see how being dissatisfied is what made the path look split, right?

Well, yeah. Being dissatisfied would make me want to create an option.

There are always endless options all along, but you would begin to bring one or more of them into focus if you didn't feel good where you were. Feeling good, by the way, is one of those wonderful gauges you've been supplied with, along with the other diving gear. So is knowing when you're hungry or full, thirsty or quenched, too hot or too cold or just right. You have a perfect instrument, although it can get clouded, with which to determine what to do next. Joy is what leads you toward those who would help you develop your talents. Joy is what beckons you to where your gifts will be most appreciated. Feeling wonderful, full of wonder, full of awe and eagerness, feeling full of life is what life is meant to feel like.

So, even if there were no fork, we'd be looking at how to get through the bramble bushes along the path if we had to, if we were feeling that dissatisfied, that lacking in joy.

Right.

And we only think there's a dilemma because once we've noticed an option, we get fearful about moving toward it, but we wouldn't have noticed it if we didn't want to move away from what we were doing. I can see that. The fork I noticed or created or focused on is the fork I don't even want to make disappear, even though I could if I wanted to. But, okay, how about if I'm feeling good, and suddenly my situation just isn't going to stay the way it was, and I look at the options, which are quite unlike the very satisfying situation that is dissolving, and I can see how either one could be okay but neither one is more appealing than the other. What do you do when you're in a gully, and two canyons branch off, and you can't go back? The posse's on your tail, or the boyfriend is in love with someone else, or your job was discontinued, or you don't have legs any more, or your child died, or…

Whoa. You're talking about serious changes. But even if they weren't that serious, you'd still have choices, only they're not the choices you think they are.

What?

You think you have to decide to go left or right.

Well, don't you?

Your choices in the situations you just mentioned are not left or right, they're staying where you are or moving forward.

You're saying it doesn't matter which direction you go in, as long as you just go in one?

I'm saying you aren't really at a fork in the road. Even if there were seven canyons, your choices are to do nothing or to do something, and doing nothing is doing something.

Okay, okay, you're saying there's no fork in the road, or even if there is, it isn't about the fork, it's about giving up or going on. My choices are to intend a change or to surrender to a change, because a change will happen. Okay, gotcha. But. What about if, say, I can see my goal. I'm in a valley, there's the tower I want to reach, and right in front of me are two paths, and it looks from here like either one is basically heading in the general direction of my goal. What then?

Well, if the goal is what's important to you, and the scenery along the way is not, what difference would it make which way you went?

Aaaahhhh!!!

You want to be told that it matters which way you go. It doesn't matter unless it does.

If it matters to me, then it matters.

Yes.

Okay! So let's say, here, then, let's say that it *matters*. I'm standing at a fork in the road. I don't know how I got here. I'm hot, I'm frustrated, I'm tired, and I need some water. There isn't any water in my canteen. How do I know which way is going to lead me to the water? I want to find the water, because if I don't, I'll die! I don't want to die! I like breathing out and breathing in, it's second nature to me now, I'm very grateful I'm alive! It *matters* that I *stay* alive. Okay? It *matters*! Which way do I go?

Your original question was, does it matter which way you go. The answer to that question is, it matters as much as you want it to. You are the one who decides how much it matters. If it mattered to your sister in the same way as the life-and-death situation you've just described, then she would go toward the smell of water. Which is what she did. When she was thirsty, she was offered a sip by someone who beckoned her to follow for more, and so she followed. Eventually she discovered something. She could make sure she herself always had her own water. She didn't have to play someone else's game to get water. So she came to, or noticed, or created, another fork in the road, and at that point, when she left the cult, she knew she could follow any direction at all because she had her own water.

Oh! You've just helped me understand something!

What's that?

There was a time in my life when I thought that I had only so much light inside, and when too many people drew it out of me, because they thought I was the source of light in their lives, I would be left in the darkness. I'd always have to retreat and replenish myself from the original source of light. It took me a long time to get that anyone could go to the original source. It took me a long time to get that I didn't have to keep giving *all* my light away until I had no more left. I could give away some of the light I'd drawn into myself during the night from the ever-abundant source, but it was easier and better to tell others how to do it for themselves. Thank you! If we know how to get our own water, we're not scared, we don't buy into need-trips or control-trips, we're just basically meeting a challenge or pursuing an adventure. But now I have another question.

Okay.

What if the fork in the road is the decision between a desert and a rain forest, but you can't tell from here which is which?

You're saying that you can replenish your supply of life-supporting nourishment in one place, but not in another?

Well…Yeah. It *is* easier to find water near a waterfall.

Do you know how a San gets water out of the African desert? Do you know how an aboriginal Australian finds water when he goes on walkabout?

No, I don't know how, exactly. I mean, I've seen and read about how, but that doesn't mean I could find water in the desert, even if they can.

The point is that they can, because they are familiar with the territory. Once you're familiar with the territory, you can choose where to go and where not to go. Getting familiar with the terrain, the physical plane, the way people interact, the ins and outs of being a material girl as well as a metaphysical one, the inner territory as well as the outer, is about becoming fluid, being able to find water in the desert or swim around in the bigger picture because you know that you and the water are the same.

True freedom is knowing that it doesn't matter which fork you take… unless it does. If it does matter to you which direction you head into, it's because you want or need to become familiar with that part of the terrain. What does the landscape look like when you're a parent, or a prisoner, or a soldier, or a celebrity, or the fifth wheel, or poverty-stricken? The more you become familiar with the terrain, the more freely you can decide how long you want to stay in one place, in that definition of yourself. You can stay there until you want to move on, into another definition of yourself, and you can move on, whether it's in the same geographical location or another one, without regrets. That's what your sister did. She didn't have to look back with bitterness; she took whatever she needed along and left the rest behind. When you have no regrets, because you know it all adds up to why you're here, to experience it, to experiment with it, to create it, to enjoy it, to love it, you won't wonder about which way to go. Nothing can trap you into permanent dissatisfaction.

Any time spent in a state of depression, confusion, exhaustion, dread, hatred, rage, or despair, is time in need of redemption. There are no sins in the Universal Light of All-knowing Love. But time lost to less than joy is time the soul will want to redeem, to embrace with love and joy, eventually, and when it does, it will know grace, and that when *can be now. You can begin in this very moment to ask yourself what it is you can do to create and experience joy. There's always a way to alter your course or tap into the source. There is always a change in the air.*

Kinda like the weather. The wind is whipping up the trees right now, blowing that humidity right off the hills, and all the papers off my desk. Ooh, just listen to that thunder roll. Change is in the air. Without me going anywhere.

Are you singing?

Oops. Sorry.

12

Making Waves

Here's a fun little exercise in the physics of consciousness. If you aren't especially thrilled by the mathematics of motion, you might not want to wade through this with me to the best part, so I'll throw some of the best part at you right away. Everything in the universe is radiating spherical waves out into everything else in the universe, and all these spherical waves are ricocheting off one another, getting superimposed on one another, creating interference patterns with one another, and in general vibrating all over the place to beat the band. All of these waves, which are called electromagnetic waves and include radio waves and x-rays, are all traveling at the speed of light. There's only one that I know of that can break the envelope, that can exceed the speed of light into the next dimensions, and it's coming from your brain.

Okay, if that enticement is enough to make you want to read on, here we go. If not, I'll see you at the other end of the roller coaster.

All the electromagnetic waves, which scientists seem to have determined travel at 186,283 miles per second, are measured in both frequencies and wavelengths.

The frequency is measured in how many crests of the wave pass a given point in one second. The wavelength is the distance between crests. The larger the wavelength is, the smaller the number indicating the frequency is, and vice versa.

To picture this, imagine your finger at the edge of a kind of lie-detector graph, which is producing a crowded row of vertical zigzags or pointed mountains. Since they're packed so close, hundreds of them are speeding past your fingertip in the span of one second. Their crest-to-crest length is short. The number of how many of them fly by is large. Now imagine a long rolling wave, so long you can't see its first crest by the time the second one shows up. In the span of a second, only a few of them pass your finger. The longer the wavelength, the smaller the number of times a crest passes your finger.

The known spectrum of electromagnetic waves begins, at one end of the scale, with cosmic waves, which range in *wavelength* from 10-to-the-minus-13 meters long, from crest to crest (I can't even imagine how teeny that is – we must be down into fractions of atomic diameters here), to 10-to-the-minus-25 meters. The *frequency* of cosmic waves ranges from 10-to-the-plus-25 to 10-to-the-plus-13 crests, or cycles, per second. (These are unimaginably huge numbers of crests zipping past our given point.) Heading from cosmic waves toward the other end of the scale, we encounter, in decreasing frequencies and increasing wavelengths, gamma rays, x-rays, ultraviolet rays, the visible light spectrum, infrared rays, radar, microwaves, TV, and the broadcast band of AM – FM radio waves, which are in the neighborhood of about 500 to 800 meters long, with a frequency in the neighborhood of a megahertz (a million crests or cycles per second).

At the other end of the scale we come to the brain waves. Beta brain waves, which are emitted during analytical interaction with the environment, range from a frequency of 30 to 18 cycles per second. They have wavelengths of several thousand miles. Alpha waves are emitted during relaxation and meditation at 12 to 7 cycles per second, and Theta waves during the creative process at 6 to 5 cycles per second, with wavelengths in the tens of thousands of miles long. (Picture the lie-detector graph producing what looks more and more like an almost straight line.)

Now we're getting to the interesting part. Delta brain waves. To my knowledge, they have been measured so far only during deep sleep and the slowed-down state that yogis can attain. If Delta brain waves had frequencies of 4 to 1 cycles per second, they would have wavelengths of about 46,500 miles to 186,283 miles. That number looks familiar because it is the speed of light, 186,283 miles per second. But Delta brain waves don't have frequencies of 4 to 1 cycles per second. They have frequencies of 4 to 0 cycles per second.

What is happening in that space between 1 and 0 cycles per second? At 1 cycle, the wavelength is, for simplicity's sake, 186,000 miles long. At one one-thousandths of a cycle, it's 186,000,000 miles long. The closer we get to zero, the longer the wavelength is, until we are so close that the wavelengths of these radiating brainwaves are approaching infinity. If we were still looking at a graph, we'd be getting nervous, because zero would look like a flat line, and we all know what flat lining means. So let's go back to remembering that in fact what is radiating from our brains are not linear but spherical waves, expanding bubbles that are growing vaster and vaster, creating interference patterns with all the other waves that everything else is emitting, and yet, like the light from the most distant quasars, finding enough space to travel through to cross the known universe and beyond.

We can reach zero and cross over into infinity in two ways. We can die, send out that last wave, after which no more will follow from that particular brain in that particular body, or we can do what the yogis do. When we still our minds completely, when we reach that absolute silence, that sense of having no personal existence, which the yogis describe as a prerequisite to enlightenment, the spherical wave that was last emitted from the brain is almost infinite in length. We are no longer relating to the frequencies at hand, creating interference patterns with our tangible environment. At that point, one second after we sent out that last brain wave, our relationship to the universe has become almost omni-present, encompassing all the frequencies of all the wavelengths being emitted by everything in an almost infinite universe. We can die into enlightenment, or we can just visit the All and return to our normal awareness by resuming the emission of shorter brain waves.

But do we have to go that far out? We are being bombarded with every frequency of every wavelength, from ultraviolet rays to the brain waves coming from the neighbor next door, all the time, all the time we're not sitting inside a lead box, anyway. Even while we are not perceptually experiencing our individual selves as the All, we can comprehend ourselves as experiencing it, as being connected to and influenced by and influencing all of it. There is no separation. We are a Oneness of Being.

And then, of course, we can filter out most of it, because it's time to take out the garbage.

13

The Artist on Loan

My favorite way to paint is to start by preparing a canvas with a variety of colors thrown into the gesso in order to form random combinations of hues and shapes. As I smooth the pigments into the gesso with a fan brush, or dab and dart a rag at the canvas, the tone or character of the background develops. It might be pale, with subtle pastels vaguely blending into one another, or dark, with smears of sienna and umber twisting around a hint of ochre here or violet there. It might be sprinklings and splatters and rag-crinkle patterns of blues and aquas and greens. By the time I have a background with some pleasing integrity, I usually have paint-covered hands as well, so I'll set the canvas up on my easel, if I've been working it on the floor, and go wash up. When I come back, the acrylics have dried, and I can now sit and look at the canvas, from about eight or ten feet away.

I will probably be sitting here for ten or fifteen minutes. This is the time during which the random background begins to suggest certain forms or scenes or relationships. If nothing demonstrates itself to me, I'll turn the canvas onto another edge. Sometimes two or three of the turnings will show me something, so I have to choose which one I like. Ah, this way has an uplifting feeling to it. Okay, so what is this painting about? The painting already knows what it's about. All I have to do is be receptive. Gradually I begin to see it. There's a cliff there. A bird flying sideways. The hint of a human profile with an animal inside it. What is the animal? I squint. Oh, it's a bear with hunched shoulders. Is there anything I need to highlight yet? Yes, I don't want to lose where that profile is. So I take a brush and outline the rust in pale blue. But the brush wants to do more, it wants to thicken the outline here, pull the paint sideways there, then splash down into a waterfall. The brush pulls my hand along one of the random shapes of the background, bringing into relief figures that I won't recognize until I step back again. It jumps into a couple of colors on the palette and spreads the paint in twirls around a corner. I don't even know what it's doing until it has finished, but when I put the brush down and retreat a few feet... Ah! It has created a shield containing overlapping bison. And now I see where a mesa will rise up if I put a bit of red-gold sky above it. This time the brush, with three colors on it, pulls itself into a rapid succession of strokes, darting and jumping. I simply watch, getting out of the way, having no desire of my own to intend anything, to impose anything of my conscious will into the work. It's almost as if something or someone else is taking over. Sometimes these strokes will be finished in a few seconds. Sometimes they dash on and around for five minutes, filling in a large area, with what, I do not know, until once again, when the brush stops, I put it into the water and step back, way back, and sit down, and look. Whole new images have been elicited from the background by the new strokes, ones that surprise and delight me when I discover them.

The painting has taken on a very definite quality by now. It's Aboriginal or Native American or perhaps African, or it has light beings and fairies and children in it, or it's a cascade of rocks and water with ancient creatures meandering through the cracks and shadows. It has begun to pull itself together, but there are empty places and loose ends. So I look again. This time my eyes see needed colors, a hint of dioxazine purple over the burnt sienna there, a dash of cerulean blue here. My mind doesn't make a decision; my eyes see what is missing. Okay, I'll try that. Yes, and that wants to happen over here, too. When I let the painting create itself, I make no mistakes. If I try to add something for effect, it usually doesn't work. The more the painting creates itself, the more delighted and excited I get. I see what it's doing! It's as if I'm looking over the shoulder of a masterful artist, being educated in techniques and enchanted by the hues.

And then, I begin to fall in love. The painting has started to nourish me. It has started to exchange something with me, messages, emotions. It's showing me another time or place by lifting away a veil, or it's revealing a hidden aspect of myself or my life, or it's summoning the symbols and entities that will be most meaningful to the person who will be drawn to this work. I have fallen into a time warp, I am living in another world, the painting and I are creation, showing itself off, caressing the senses, becoming music, moving the secrets of the universe into visibility. Touches of the brush to the canvas are shocks of delight. Gentling the tones into softer, smoother blends is an act of affection. The character of the painting imbues me with its focus and strength, if it is a stalker, or with its wispy layers of visions, if it is a magician. It turns me into what it wants to become, so that if I am to bring out a look of wonder on the face of a child, I cannot determine what line to accent or what shadow to deepen, I can only let the sense of wonder that has overtaken me move my hand with the brush toward the right color, and then soften that color into the cheek or brow.

At least a third of the time that I am painting is spent across the room, looking for and seeing what is needed next. There comes a moment, then, after an hour, a day, or a couple of weeks, when the painting feels finished.

But two more things will still happen before it's decidedly completed.

The first is that I will sit, not to study, not to be summoned, but to receive, to allow the vision to give me back some of the energy I've put into it. This is such a replenishment that even if I have been at the canvas for the past sixteen hours and it's three o'clock in the morning, I will happily absorb for another hour what I'm being given, insights, beauty, love, empowerment, satisfaction, joy. I will continue to take in from the painting until I have received enough to be able to let it go -- to sell it or give it to someone else -- or until I've discovered that, well, this painting belongs to me.

The second thing that happens is that a day or two later, a few more additional touches will be required. Then when there is absolutely no spot left that doesn't feel exactly right, I put my little symbol in the corner, and paint the edges, or frame it, satisfied that the pleasure and love I have exchanged with it will quietly radiate itself into someone's home, over time. It's as if the number of hours condensed into the painting will gradually seep into the consciousness of the observers, they will sense the messages and emotions, subtly, if they only glance at it occasionally, more noticeably if they look awhile and let it speak itself to them as it spoke itself to me.

Although this is my favorite way to paint, there are other ways. Sometimes a scene, from my travels or from a magazine or a photo, will inspire the mood and background. A commissioned portrait, of course, will require more intention. The knowledge of who the recipient will be most definitely affects the images and tones.

One morning I finished a painting for a couple of friends who were recently married. Even though I'd chosen the scene of this gift from a photograph, a sense of what would speak to these two people created the spiritual hopefulness and contentment on the face of the Tibetan-looking man, who gazes upward beside a great plume of smoke rising from an entwined shaft of leaves. Within the smoke several winged beings and a couple appeared, without my intention. I was pleased with the final result.

As I was getting ready to leave, to deliver the painting, I asked my daughter what she thought of it. Fawni's feedback is usually a ravingly positive response, occasionally tempered with an added suggestion about highlighting something here or there. This time she said, in a somewhat solemn, actually almost frowning, voice, "Mmh...I like it better when you have more going on, like in this whole area." She indicated three-fourths of the canvas.

"Mm," I nodded. "Actually, there is quite a bit going on there, it just takes a while to see it. I could probably define more if I had the time, but I'm taking this over to them now." I wasn't displeased with her comment. I was a little surprised that she didn't like it, but we have an understanding. We're just honest with each other. So I was more than a little perplexed when she came out of her bedroom a few minutes later, with tears glistening in her eyes, and said, "Mom, I had this deep... uhn... *feeling*... when I criticized your painting..."

"Oh, Fawni!" I went to hug her, thinking she was reacting extremely sensitively with totally unnecessary regret. "I didn't think you were being too cri..."

"No, Mom, wait, let me finish! I had this *strong... feeling...*" she groped for the right words. "Harry was, like, inside me." She was talking about my father, who was an internationally acclaimed sculptor and designer. He died in 1978, a year and a half before Fawni was born. "He was... I understood him... He didn't mean to be so critical! He was telling me... he's telling me... he always criticized you three children because he knew how good you were. He was never critical with anyone else because it didn't matter to him if they weren't doing their best. He knew how good you kids were. He wanted you to do your best. But he didn't know how much he was hurting you. I want you to understand… he wants you to understand that he never meant to hurt you. He is so proud of how good you are!" Tears were streaming from her eyes.

I nodded. "I know I'm good," I smiled through my own prickling tears.

She couldn't stop crying. "He would have been… he is… so proud of his grandchildren, too."

"Oh, yes! Yes, he would have been so proud of all of you!" I was still thinking in terms of the past. Harry died when Eric was five, before the births of both of his granddaughters, Fawni and Val's daughter Kyndi. He never knew the girls. It hadn't fully hit me yet that Fawni was speaking in the present tense.

"Mom, I feel him, like he's here, helping me to understand, to look at life through his eyes. He's giving me some of his wisdom and his power."

"Oh…!" It was finally sinking in. "Oh, Fawni!" I didn't know what to say. "I'm so glad!"

We hugged. I finally understood.

My father still loves us all.

It's never too late for love.

For some reason, my friend Sue cried, too, when she saw the painting. (And here I thought it wasn't all that bad.) But then, she's been so happy lately, she cries about almost everything. It's really beautiful to see that.

It wasn't the first time someone cried over one of my paintings. A few years ago I had arranged to meet with a woman in her thirties who had opened a New Age shop. Oh, yes, she'd be delighted to have some of my paintings on her walls, she said, looking at a few photos, and if they sold, so much the better for both of us. A few days later I unloaded three or four paintings from my van, brought them into the store, leaned them against the counter, and went back out for the rest of them.

When I came back in, she was on her knees in front of one of them. She glanced up at me, wiping tears from her cheeks. "It's him," she said softly. The painting was of a Native American looking directly at us through squinting eyes. His hand was raised, and his fingertips glowed with light where they pierced the veil between him and the viewer. "He came to me again in a meditation last week, and this time I could see him really clearly," she said. "He told me that very soon I would see him, like, for real, not just in my mind, but out here. This is him! This is his face!" We both got goosebumps. "It's my spirit guide!"

I had painted that painting several years before, sensing the spirit of a Native American blending with me as I did. I'd thought the spirit was another aspect of myself, or the memory of a past life. I hadn't even considered the possibility that he had his own identity and was touching more than one life from the other side. I began to suspect that I wasn't necessarily the only one doing the painting when I painted.

My friend Marilyn dropped in with a friend of hers to show him my artwork. I wasn't home, but Fawni invited them in. Marilyn relayed to me later that her friend loved my work and would like to commission a portrait of his wife and daughter. He would send photos.

Long before the photos arrived, I felt driven to start the painting. Her friend had mentioned to Marilyn that he would like a forest, a waterfall, and some ferns in the background. Even though I was imposing these images onto the canvas, I began to see other forms emerging from the foliage. There was a mossy man, lying on the ground, with his head down, reaching blindly through the waterfall, and a leafy woman, sitting up, looking at him across the water, reaching toward him as if to comfort him. I wondered if my client had been despondent when he met his wife.

What I had intended as some bushes overhanging a low cliff and catching the sunlight took on the form of a yellow-headed parrot. I didn't get it. A parrot?

The next day, I received a phone call from my client. "Marilyn told me you've started the painting. How exciting! I got the photos together, and I was wondering, if it wouldn't be too much trouble, could you put my parrot into the painting as well? She's green with a yellow head."

"I think your parrot is already in the painting." I told him, with a sense of eerie wonder.

I had almost finished the background, leaving a blank area in the stream in front of the waterfall, by the time the photos arrived. Excited by the way the painting had been evolving, I began working on the figures of mother and child. I placed the lovely young woman, draped in an off-white dress, by the edge of the stream. She was stooping, the folds of her dress draped across her bent knees, and holding her hand out to steady the little girl standing in the water.

I stepped back from the painting.

There was another child sitting in the mother's lap. The image was somehow formed by the subtle shadows of pastel blues and pinks in the draping of the dress.

That's weird, I thought. I'd better get that out of there. I painted over it and stepped back. It was still there. I smoothed my brush into the white paint on my palette and dabbed at the dress again. That should do it. I stepped back.

There was still a child sitting in the mother's lap.

Marilyn and I had both been invited to a friend's house the next evening, and while the other ladies were talking, I sat down next to her on the couch and said in a low voice, "Marilyn, about your friend..." I whispered his name. "Is there another child in the picture?"

"Hoh!" she gasped. "What do you mean?" She looked apprehensive, as if I were spooking her by knowing some secret I wasn't supposed to know.

"I'm sorry, I don't mean to pry. I was just wondering, because there's another child in the painting, and I can't paint it out." I described what had happened, and I could tell by the way she was rubbing the goosebumps on her arms that something odd was going on.

"She recently had a miscarriage."

"Oh, my, I'm so sorry, I didn't know." It seemed that child's spirit was still around. I told Marilyn about the other images. She confirmed that her friend had indeed been despondent when he and his wife found each other.

I didn't know why I was getting these visual messages, but when I pointed them out to my client, he became more receptive to other visual messages, to the on-going conversation Life is having with us about its infinite variety of intertwining meanings. He also became one of my most ardent patrons, seeing me through several of my financially meager times with yet another commission.

Marilyn's daughter, when she commissioned a portrait of Marilyn, asked if I could add a likeness of Marilyn's mother Dorothy to the surprise birthday gift. Dorothy died when Marilyn was in her twenties, and the only reference available was an old once-crumpled, black-and-white photo, two inches square. I had to get out my magnifying glass to discern the features on Dorothy's quarter-inch-sized face.

As I painted, I asked Dorothy, whom I knew to be around, because she'd been dropping pennies into our lives (pennies from heaven, confirmation of her awareness of our prayers) to help me achieve a likeness. It seemed to be happening, the features seemed to be painting themselves, but I ran into a problem. I had positioned Dorothy above Marilyn, and I had intended that she be looking down on her daughter, but the eyes seemed to paint themselves looking up, and no matter what I did, I couldn't change that. I gave up. Dorothy wanted to be looking up at the Light above her, even though her hand was reaching down, dropping pennies around her daughter.

When Marilyn saw the painting, she was astounded. "How did you do this? This is my mother! But she isn't the age she was as I remember her. She's older. She looks like she would have if she had lived longer. How can this be?"

Some time later, Marilyn, caught up in a difficult situation, was feeling stressed and in need of inspiration. She had been hoping to find the pennies that had so often reassured her of her mother's comforting presence, on the carpet she'd just finished vacuuming, or on a chair beside a book she'd just put there a few minutes ago, but none had appeared. One afternoon her son came to the house looking for her. Not knowing if Marilyn was home, he peeked into her room, and stopped in his tracks, stunned. Dorothy was standing at the foot of the bed, looking at the painting. He knew it was his grandmother, because it was the same woman who was in the painting. He fled from the house, and didn't summon the courage to tell Marilyn about it until a day later. Marilyn was heart-warmed and grateful to know that her mother was still with her.

Help comes through from the other side in so many ways – and knows how to make good use of us on this side.

My favorite way of painting – allowing random shapes and colors to tell their story in gradually comprehended imagery, allowing myself to be an artist on loan – seems like a good metaphor for how to receive what life is trying to tell me, if I will only listen! There are so many ways in which we are being contacted, by souls who have left their bodies, by spiritual guides, by the great binary language of creation behind and within all of what is going on around us. We can be intenders if we want to be, or pretenders or offenders or defenders, for that matter, but we can also be attenders, simply present when the presents are all opened.

14

Their World

By the time June would arrive, I would remember even more of the reasons I ended up staying in Pennsylvania as long as I did. There seemed to be nothing to compare with waking up in the morning to the sweet, delicate fragrance of wild roses. It made me want to breathe and breathe. I just couldn't get enough of that sweetness, that freshness, into my body. The roses were everywhere, cascades of white blossoms perfuming the air, along the roads, draped over fences, lacing themselves up into the trees, lining the fields, creating a garden all over the countryside. The subtle aroma drifted into the window of my car, made me feel heady with promises fulfilled as I picked up the mail, and pulled me outside after dinner, to breathe it in again, because this must be what heaven smells like.

And then there were the lighted concerts in the evenings, the lightning bugs hovering and twinkling like so many fallen stars, over the fields, up into the trees, and across the pond, where the bullfrogs roared.

Bullfrogs are ancient beings, I'm now convinced, who have practiced their music for eons. The bullfrogs in that pond, at any rate, had it down pat.

I sat by the pond one evening long enough to discover something I'd never noticed before. I'd always thought that those twilight concerts were just a jumble of randomly contributed bellows and groans. After a few minutes, however, I began to *hear* what I'd been listening to: the pattern, the rhythm of their symphony.

This particular evening's selection starts with one deep, grandfatherly *rrhuaogh*, low, slow, and mournful, from the wet black roots of that overhanging maple tree. After four seconds of silence, from among the reeds at the shallow end come two sounds, a little perkier, similar to rubbing a balloon with a thumb, *bruigh, bruigh*, so close together that it has to be two frogs. Three seconds pass, and now three relatively high plunks, like rubber bands snapping, *bleghit, bleghit, bleghit*, sound from three different places on the circumference of the pond.

After a long moment of silence, the same *rrhuaogh*, low, slow, and mournful, sounds again from the roots of the maple. Four seconds go by, and then, from the reeds, *bruigh, bruigh*. After three seconds I hear *bleghit, bleghit, bleghit* from the same three different places around the pond. This time a few tenors and basses, perhaps five or six of them, chorus in from different locations. After a moment of silence, the theme begins again. *Rrhuaogh. Bruigh, bruigh. Bleghit, bleghit, bleghit*, and now, after the five or six, a variety of tenors and basses join in from everywhere, gradually building to a Didjeridoo-like droning chorus, a many-layered operatic tale of life in the primeval mud, of earth before man, of warnings from the elders about snappers in the murky depths, of sorrow, endurance, and harmony, deep hollow gravelly sounds, low, slow, mournful *rrhuaorrghs* underneath the boings and blips, building to an almost frenzied crescendo in slow motion, and then, suddenly, abruptly, *silence*. The pond is serene in the moonlight, the fireflies are soundlessly reflected in the water, a gentle breeze barely whispers through the silvery leaves of the trees. Then, from the roots of that maple rolls a single heavy sound: *rrhuaogh*, low, slow, and mournful. *Bruigh, bruigh. Bleghit, bleghit, bleghit*. Silence. *Rrhuaogh. Bruigh, bruigh*. And after the third round, everyone joins in again, and builds to a bellowing rumble of circular sound, longer and deeper and higher and more so, until: silence.

A bullfrog could probably tell you whether or not the theme of the symphony varies from round to round, or night to night, or year to year, but I'm very proud of myself for being able to report as much discernment as I have. Bullfrogs have some kind of wisdom that I can't fathom, but I do know what they've got going when it comes to concerts. They have an ear for music. If you come upon a frog quietly, so that he isn't startled by your evidently dangerous clumsiness, and start to talk to him, or sing to him, he will by all means sit and listen, quite transfixed, actually, as your voice is probably intriguingly unlike all the other sounds in his world, including the birdcalls. Of course, since it's been their reactions to *my* singing that I've witnessed, that transfixed gaze could conceivably be dumbstruck horror.

Even the tadpoles are sensitive to sound. (Of course this was obvious as soon as it occurred to me – what isn't obvious is why it didn't occur to me sooner.) Bullfrogs are about as big as your hand, and their tadpoles, who take two years to grow legs, are huge, as tadpoles go. I hate to say it, but they look like they're meant to be eaten. Fat juicy morsels of pure boneless gold-green protein, jellied dumplings with tails, which the turtles and the heron must find absolutely delectable. I'm sorry, but there are hundreds, if not thousands, of them in this pond, and if they all grew up into concert aficionados, the uproar could be deafening, so it's just as well that some of them slide down somebody's gullet.

How I found out about them being so plentiful and having ears was accidental. But now that I know, I've shared it with others.

My step-daughter Raine and her son Eli and I stand on the little patch of sandy shore by the pond. It is late afternoon.

"Ready?" says Eli.

"Ready."

"One, two, three, *clap!*" The three of us clap our hands together loudly, once, and across the expanse of the pond we see hundreds of little splashes, as if someone has just thrown widely scattered handfuls of gravel that kerplunk into the water. "One, two, three, *clap!*" It feels like magic. Stand by the pond, clap or shout suddenly and briefly, and everywhere you look, hundreds of mini-fountains arise in unison out of nowhere. I don't know what those tadpoles are doing, flipping their tails as they dive for cover, leaping up to see what's happening, dude, or just getting blasted out of their juicy little morsel wits, but whatever it is, they will keep on doing it for five or six more claps, and then the splashes diminish in number, until nobody's all that excited anymore.

Meanwhile, who knows what great-grandmother bullfrog thinks of all this, watching us invisibly from her haven in the sunlit tea-colored water near the mossy bank. I haven't seen a frog shake her head or roll her eyes yet. But maybe they'll all sing about it later this evening.

I have known animals to offer their vocal tributes specifically to humans. Some years ago, Fawni's friend Gwenn, who'd moved in with us for a few months until she and her boyfriend could find their own place, gave birth to a little girl. On Zaliah's first morning in our house, I was awakened by an odd sound outside the window. Finally I recognized it. A flock of about thirty wild turkeys occasionally crossed our field down near the edge of the woods. Once or twice I'd seen a few brave toms and hens come as close as the driveway. But I'd never seen this. On the brick patio, right outside of Gwenn's bedroom, were two female turkeys, bobbing their heads and clucking toward the newborn and her mother inside. They continued to cluck and gobble gently for about five minutes, bowing their heads beneath the window, as if it were a manger.

That was the only time that such a welcome, such a tribute, had been offered us by any of the turkeys (whom I'd like to rename with something more elegant-sounding, like peacock or swan or secretary bird, something that would elevate them from future dinner to the tall, graceful, stately beings that they are, as much of a thrill to witness in their displays of shimmering fanned feathers as any other exotic, free-roaming monarchs of the wild).

June is also the time of year that the fawns are born. My daughter Fawni was named after a fawn that her father was raising when I met him. When Fawni was four and Eric was eleven, they both asked me if we could go find a fawn. Okay, I shrugged, figuring a walk through the woods and fields would be a nice way to spend an early summer afternoon. We breathed in the fragrance of the honeysuckle and picked daisies and startled pheasants into flight and gnawed the bark of beech-nut-gum-flavored twigs. We meandered along a path through the woods and climbed up on an old stump and squatted in front of convoluted mushrooms growing on tree trunks. We crumpled lemon-smelling mitten-shaped leaves and rubbed them on our wrists, to keep the mosquitoes away, and looked up at the blue jays squawking overhead.

By the time we turned toward home, we had forgotten our original mission, so I almost tripped over my own feet at the unexpected sight, gasping in my effort not to step on the little creature hidden beneath some May-apple fronds. Curled up so compactly it could have fit on a dinner plate, its tiny domed head resting on a dainty knee, the fawn's beauty made us croon in awe. We knelt beside it, and before I could stop them, the children were cooing and petting its fluffy red white-spotted fur. It lifted its moist black nose, twitched its translucent ears, and blinked its long-lashed blue-brown eyes at us in total trust.

"Can we take it home?" Fawni begged.

"Please, Ma?" Eric joined in.

"But its mother must be somewhere close," I told them.

"But what if she's not?"

"Oh, Ma, please!"

"I always wanted a fawn!"

"It would be so cool, Ma. Look, she doesn't mind being picked up." Eric had grasped her gently in a hug and was standing up. Her long legs draped down to his knees.

"Can I carry her?" Fawni prodded, grasping her neck.

"Oh, be careful!" I cried, knowing how the two of them could get carried away about whatever they both wanted. Thinking it was too late now anyway, the mother would never accept our smell on her, I gently took the fawn from Eric's arms, and fell in love.

The children petted her as we walked home. They named her Flower. They prepared a bedding of grass in a cardboard box under the desk in my bedroom. They tried to give her milk from an old baby bottle, but she wasn't interested. They caressed her and talked to her and told her she was beautiful.

Finally they went to sleep, but I couldn't, not with this amazingly present little being in my room. She tried to stand up, and after a struggle, she managed to do so, for the first time, I suspected, which meant she hadn't even nursed yet. I tried the baby bottle again. She didn't want to have anything to do with it. She cried. The sound broke my heart. I was sure her mother was crying for her, too. Then she settled down and rested her chin on her forelegs, with infinite, innocent patience.

I tried to sleep, but there was a sound in the atmosphere that I couldn't identify, a distant drumbeat. Suddenly I knew what it was. I crept close to the fawn. It was her heart. It was beating so loudly it filled the room, maybe even the forest beyond. Maybe her mother could hear it.

I'll take you back in the morning, I promised her in silence.

As soon as it was light enough to see, I carried her to where we'd found her and prayed that her mother needed Flower as much as Flower needed her.

The children were both disappointed, but sympathetic, when I explained that Flower just wouldn't take the milk, and how would they feel if someone took them away from their mom? I knew how I would feel if someone took my babies away from me. They went together to the woods, and came back to report that Flower wasn't where I'd left her. We were hopeful. Why wouldn't a doe want her newborn and be back to check again? Human smell or not, couldn't she sense that we had meant no harm? We assured one another that Flower's mother would know we had loved her baby and were grateful for our time with her. We were sure she had come back for her because she loved her, too.

I wondered if we'd ever know if that was true.

Two weeks later, as we were driving past the field near that patch of woods, Eric shouted, "Ma! Stop the car! Stop the car!" Fawni and I watched as he bolted from the minivan and dashed across the field. As he slowed down, we saw what he was approaching. In the tall golden grass under a few dark pines stood a small red fawn. He walked up to her, to within two feet of her, so close he could have reached out and touched her, and stood quietly and spoke to her. She flicked her tail and ears at him. We were out of hearing distance, so we didn't know what Eric was saying. After a few minutes, he slowly reached out his hand, but she backed up a step. He straightened up and spoke to her again. She seemed to nod, and then shake her head, and then she turned, not in a hurry, just letting him know she was free now, as she trotted slowly into the shade, all feminine angles and bounce. He stood there for another moment, saying something as the fawn paused and turned her head to look at him once more before ambling into the forest. He walked slowly back across the field. Fawni and I were all ears, bursting with eager questions that were silenced by the lovely look on his face.

"It was Flower," he said, beaming softly. "She recognized her name."

It is such a privilege to be allowed into the world of a wild animal, to be given the opportunity to respect its sensitivity.

A couple of years after we'd been blessed by Flower, a friend called and said he'd found a nest of baby raccoons in his attic. He was going to put them in a box, put it outside for the mother to find, and seal up his attic. If we'd ever wanted a raccoon as a pet, now was our chance.

Well, we had to go and see them, at least. There were six of them, an unusually large litter for a raccoon, each barely bigger than a thumb. Their eyes were still shut. After the experience with the fawn, there was no way I'd want to risk having a wild baby refuse cow's milk, but it just so happened that Eric's cat Mimi had just had kittens. So we slipped two tiny snub-nosed aliens in with her litter and rolled them around a bit to get them to smell familiar. We needn't have taken the precaution. Mimi responded to their funny whirring whines by licking them both profusely and rolling herself over so they could find her nipples.

They were still nursing from her when they were as big as she was. The kittens were a third their size. Mimi, the best mother cat we ever knew, bathed and batted them all with the same loving attention. Fawni and my stepson Luke, who were both six years old at the time, took particular delight in setting their unfinished bowls of cereal out by the picnic table. The kittens would dash across the lawn to lap up the milk, and Girl and Coon would lumber over almost as hastily to fish for floating cheerios. Coon would swim his black paws exploringly through the milk, scoop up a cheerio, delicately pop it in under his pointy black nose, and then, while nonchalantly sniffing the air and looking around with his bright black eyes, as if enjoying the view of the clouds, he would wipe his paws on the back of one of the kittens, using her as a napkin and paying no attention whatsoever to our appreciative laughter.

He learned how to open the screened door. It wasn't enough to let *himself* in, he'd hold the door open until Girl and every one of the kittens had entered the living room before him, and then he'd lumber into the kitchen and try to pull open the refrigerator door as well. The six-year-olds were a lot more thrilled about that than I was.

When the family returned from a week's vacation, during which time my mother had stopped in to feed the animals, Girl was gone. We didn't know if she'd wandered off or been seduced by some other raccoon or what. Coon was so much bigger than the young cats by then that they'd become intimidated by his rough-housing and would generally head for the hills with their tails whipping when he attempted to engage them in play.

He must have been getting lonely for company. He'd been leaning against my ankle as I sat on a lawn chair in the twilight enjoying the fireflies, but when I reached down to pat him, he rolled out of reach and started dashing around under the chair, teasing me hopefully. I laughed and joined him on the lawn. He whirred excitedly at my acceptance of his invitation, and began to charge and withdraw, huffing himself up and then disappearing behind me as I turned around on hands and knees. He bounced forward and nipped at my hair playfully. I ducked my head under my arms, and he crawled up on my back and grabbed my hair and slid down and excitedly nipped me on the shoulder. I let out a squeal, not so much because it hurt, but because I wanted to let him know I wasn't into getting that rough. He stopped instantly, turned to where he had nipped me, and licked the spot. I'd never been licked by a raccoon before. Unlike cat's cheese-grater tongues, raccoons' are as smooth and soothing as a puppy's. Then he patted me with his soft-padded little hands, as if to ask if all was forgiven. I had learned not to reach for the top of his head to pet him. He'd always duck away. If I reached for his hands, he'd offer me one. Yes, all is forgiven, Coon. Can you forgive me for trapping you halfway between tame and wild, with none of your own kind to be with?

When he got older, he took to wandering. I hoped he was finding other raccoons who'd teach him the tricks of survival in the woods, but he'd almost always come back late at night for handouts. He'd thrived on cat kibble and leftovers, so I knew he enjoyed a variety of snacks. I wasn't sure what he was trying to tell me one October night when he politely accepted an old favorite, a cold hot dog, put it down beside him, and then reached his hands up again. I went back into the house and brought out a slice of bread. That joined the hot dog on the grass beside him, and up came the hands again. He looked at me intently. And then, I'm not sure how, it struck me. I brought him a raw egg. He stretched tall before I'd even started to bend toward him, graciously accepted the egg, and hunched off with it in his mouth to the edge of the lawn, where he broke it open and slurped it up. He came back and stood up, paws extended, eager for another. After two more, I told him that was all for now. He looked at me with his bright dark eyes, reached his hands up to touch mine, bent down and collected the hot dog and piece of bread, took them off to the edge of the lawn, where he finished them off, and then meandered off into the woods that had, I thought, become his home.

One November morning, the children told me there was a raccoon outside the front door. I opened it and was surprised to find Coon sleeping by the woodpile. He looked so big and healthy and bushy and serene, anyway, that I thought he was just sleeping. I should have guessed that he hadn't found his favorite food to be eggs, in October, in the wild. I'm assuming he began to bother the farmers in the area, and someone set out poison. He'd known something was amiss, and he'd come home, to what he considered home, after all, to die.

I never mourned another animal friend as deeply. I'd never felt so much guilt intertwined with feeling so honored. It's a difficult question – the one about whether or not to teach wild animals to trust human beings, when there are still human beings who can't be trusted to respond to a sensitive being in a four-legged body. At least there's no question any more that animals are sensitive. There are more and more humans, finally, or again, recognizing and resounding with that truth, and that's a wonderful thing. For it is their world, too, the fawns' and the frogs', and mine wouldn't be the same without them.

15

Filter or Non-filter

More often than I like to admit, certain people appear to me to be incredibly obtuse. Manipulative. Arrogant. Insincere. Twisted. Or so perpetually redundant I want to open up their skulls, put in a new CD, and keep my remote handy (like some manipulative, arrogant, twisted, redundant egomaniac). Some of these personalities are more challenging than others when it comes to regarding them as versions of the original Star Performer, so I've been collecting some filters to keep in my back pocket for pseudo-emergencies. Because even though the world is perfect just as it is (I mean, where else in the universe that we know of can we find such a variety of choices for souls who want to explore the terrain?), I like that we're actually considering becoming a global family, one where everybody can move on from the two-year-old tantrums about what belongs to whom and who can't do what, and into the excitement of sharing our fun and our responsibilities. I want to take part in that responsibility. I don't want to lose sight of that Amazing Face looking back at me through all these different pairs of eyes.

A recent phone call, however, had me desperately resisting that remote control and scrambling through my entire collection of ways to regard others as reflections of the One.

One of my filters I stumbled upon accidentally years ago.

I had taken an empty seat and was looking around the room at the two dozen or so people waiting for the workshop to begin, and because I didn't know who the speaker was, I wondered if he or she might already be in the room, talking to someone or waiting until things settled down before taking the podium. As I looked around at all the faces, to my growing wonderment, I could see in each face the potential for a master teacher. That tired-looking, too-thin woman – I could see her getting up in front of the room, beaming a smile of wisdom upon us, and proceeding to offer us invaluable insights. That teenaged boy, despite his acne, might already have been to the other side and returned with some knowing that would ignite a memory in all of us. That voluminous man could be a healer, guided by Love to rid us of prejudices and heighten our frequencies. That man with the down-turned mouth, perhaps he'd been through a war and his unguarded face still expressed the deep sorrow that had transformed him into an angel of peace. Only one of these people was going to go to the front of the room and assume the role of teacher, while the rest of us would presume ourselves to be students, but as I looked around, I understood how interchangeable the roles were. The only difference between the speaker and the listeners would be the drive and the confidence to articulate into a meaningful story the impact of a unique life experience that could edify us all.

After happening upon this filter which high-lighted the masterful wisdom behind each physical facade, I was given another one which high-lighted the facade, the mask, by my children and my step-children, both the ones who stayed behind the scenes, on evenings such as this, and the ones who stepped forth to entertain the adults lounging in the living room.

The younger children would come down the hall from the bathroom, where they'd been giggling for five minutes, and present themselves to the people in the living room, in adult clothes: high heels, dresses dragging, suit pants crumpled to the floor over polished business shoes. The audience, the rest of the family and whatever friends might have dropped in, would utter impressed oohs and ahs. The kids would be shyly pleased with our reactions and then go traipsing back to the bathroom, only to reappear a few minutes later in black capes and scary masks and wigs, which would elicit gasps and exclamations of dread. Satisfied with their impact, they'd disappear again. A few minutes later we would be treated to clowns with painted faces, and our laughter would be genuinely hilarious, having finally been appropriate to release. Whatever the children's innovation, it was our delightful duty to be duly responsive.

So, sometimes when I just can't seem to see through the mask that someone's wearing over her Godface, I don't even try to – I can just look at the mask and enjoy it for what it is, experimentation, drama, entertainment, a physical expression donned by a Self othering Itself to get a reaction from Itself, and what a spoilsport I would be if I couldn't get into being scared or impressed or fooled or sympathetic.

A third filter presented itself to me during a pseudo-emergency (one of those times when the defense system gets activated by out-dated settings and up come the judgements, accusations, deceptions, denials, and other alarm-reactive countermeasures that set the stage for enemy interaction instead of harmonious recognition of differences.) This filter transforms my perception of grown people into children, into pre-socialized toddlers who interact in a raw, immediate, and mostly non-verbal way.

I found myself in a situation involving two women who each wanted to work on different projects with my brother without the involvement of the other woman. As an unwitting participant in a game of mistrust, I was having trouble seeing how I could disentangle myself. We were all acting like pre-language babies in a playground. Oh! How, exactly, would that scenario play out? I adjusted the filter over my lens of perception and took a look.

Here in a sandbox squats a one-and-a-half-year-old version of fifty-one-year-old Val, building something with some pebbles. Little curly-haired Missy, the toddler version of her thirty-something self, is adding pebbles to what little Val is building, and he seems quite content with her additions. Another little girl with straight hair (the pre-school self of a forty-something woman) would like to add something, too, and little Val accepts her joining in, but curly-haired Missy sits back and frowns, and at the placement of a second pebble, pushes away the hand of straight-haired little Milly. When Milly backs away, frowning, and starts to build something with the pebbles very close to the first design, Missy pushes the sand out to claim an area for her and Val to expand in.

Milly, with a frown, begins to rebuild her own design a little further away. Along comes another toddler, a little blonde girl (me). Milly offers a pebble to the passing newcomer, who stops, squats beside her, and watches what she's doing. Little blonde Lesta picks up one of the pebbles from Milly's design, examines it, and offers it to her brother. Milly frowns and tries to grab little Lesta's arm back, but Lesta jerks her arm away and puts the pebble into her brother's design. Milly is upset. Lesta is upset. Missy and Val are upset. Four chubby tots are wailing in the sandbox.

What can the adult observer do? As the adult observer, I don't have a clue, but little blonde Lesta stands up with a seriously determined set to her down-turned little lips, looks around at all the pebbles in all the other sandboxes, and toddles off, leaving the other three children to do whatever they want to with the pebbles in that one.

The solution I found by remaining in that pre-language state long enough to let my uncensored feelings emerge was the one that seemed to suit me best at the time, although there may have been others. Meanwhile, as the adult observer, I'd been able to regard with impartiality my own part in the conflict, as well as all of our parts, our roles, our Godself's ways of expressing different degrees of separation and connectedness, of scarcity and abundance, of illusion and reality, as S/H/We will.

I had already used all three filters, for years, with a woman who considered me her friend. (What I was beginning to consider her was not as commendable.) I could see the lonely only child looking for a sibling. I could see what the wise woman behind the facade of neediness was teaching me. Long-enduring, selfless, considerate patience. (The same kind of patience I thought I'd already learned when my daughter at age three fell in love with an album of Christmas songs and wanted to play the entire album seventeen times a day, every day, in January. "It's beginning to look a lot like Christmas," sung by the Pound Puppies in howling barks and whines, doesn't even appeal to my senses once, in December.) I could also see how well this woman was playing her part. She was getting every reaction she wanted to get from me. I was a bottomless pit of reactions. I was an unlimited-mileage free-gas no-deposit-no-rental-fee limousine of sensitive, comforting, insincere reactions. Finally, when the gamut of my reactions was about to be turned over, like an odometer, to all zeroes again, I told her, in a way Saint Peter would most certainly have chewed his eraser over as he studied the log of my life, that I had learned *enough*, we *weren't* sisters, and I was *tired* of reacting.

This brave woman recently risked another possibly annihilating response and called me again, hoping, I assume, that a margin-of-safety cool-down period of two years had been sufficient time for me to overhaul my limo.

I went silent, as in brain dead, for fifteen entire minutes, occasionally staring with incredulity at the same recording I'd heard for years coming through the receiver. I glanced around helplessly. I checked my back pockets. I was out of filters.

I need a new filter!

What could I have done differently?

She finally stopped talking, wondering if there was anyone home.

Instead of a few mumbled monotone responses, repetitions of earlier ineffective ones, maybe I could have said, "Hi, You-ni-verse."

"What?" (I imagine would be her response.)

Okay, I can't be totally insensitive to the fact that she's describing what she experiences as very unfortunate and difficult. I can't say, "Hi, You-ni-verse, great job!" Can I? How would she take that?

"What do you mean?"

"Great job. You're doing a great job." I wouldn't just be saying that, either, I'd mean it, really, though maybe not in the same way she'd be hearing it. It's not that I don't have compassion for what she's been experiencing. It's just that she's been experiencing it for so many years, I'd like to see something change, for her sake as well as mine.

She's not cynical, just insecure, so maybe she'd say, "Oh. Why, thank you."

"You're welcome. Gotta go. 'Bye," is what would work for me, but I don't see her as someone who can pick up on a subtle hint. I imagine she'd want to know why I was calling her You-ni-verse, and then I'd feel like I'd have to be her limousine again, taking her over the same old roads, which I don't want to be bothered taking the time to do, because that hasn't made any difference in the past, none that I could see, anyway, which is why I'm struggling here.

"I don't understand what you meant by calling me Universe."

"Well, if you were the Universe, the Source, God, what would you be telling yourself about your situation right now?" Ooh, that might work. Then all I'd have to do every time she strayed from being God would be to... leave the driving to her. She'd come up with something, because even if she didn't think she had an answer, she's the one who does. She is God. Duh. Now *that's* a filter! No, wait – it's the ultimate non-filter. It filters out all the interference patterns entirely. Why didn't I ever think of that before?

16

All the Same

My friend and website partner David, who is a spiritual counselor, was asked through his website how we can know whether or not a soul is advanced. How *can* we know, we wondered, since we don't even know how long the life of a soul might be?

When my son Eric was ten, he paused among his Legos and stared off into some other dimension and uttered a mesmerizing monologue, in which he described the arrival of souls to the planet, both physically and spiritually, from elsewhere. He said, among other things, that a human lifetime is just one day in the life of a soul.

Since human lifetimes can range from a few seconds to over a hundred years, maybe the lives of souls are that varied in length of time as well. Maybe the separation from the Source is brief for some and almost eternal for others.

Maybe there's no way to determine the advancement or age of a soul any more than there's a way to determine whether or not that apparently innocent child knows more about the relationships going on around her than that apparently sophisticated adult who has studied relationships for years. Maybe some souls, like some people, seem to know a lot about what's going on because they've been here many times, experimenting with life on Earth. David pointed out that living on this plane, within the motion of time, does have its limits and requirements. Someone in Kindergarten can't drive a car. Someone in third grade can't build a house. We do have to go through certain progressions to advance our mastery of reality. But the evolutionary position of a soul, though it might be deduced by the light that shines from within, certainly isn't dependent on evident age or appearance or ability. Meanwhile, those souls who've returned to Earth many times might still be less knowledgeable on another planet in some other part of the universe. And maybe some souls who appear to be new or young or clueless are simply visiting here, as a human, for the first time, although somewhere else they might have had quite a handle on things.

Maybe some souls like individuating so much that they come back into a human body again and again, not just because of karma, payback, lessons, purpose, or evolution toward enlightenment, but because it's fascinating or fun or compelling, less boring than seventy million other planets, and they've been on the waiting list for eons because this is one exciting place to be.

There could be as many reasons for a soul to live where it does, the way it does, for as long as it does, as there are reasons for human beings to do so. More, even.

There could also be as many reasons for a soul to cease individuation and dissolve into the All as there are for people to die to this particular lifetime.

And if that has any plausibility, then what happens when a soul is not in a body could be infinitely varied as well. Life after death could be seven billion different experiences for our present population. A few samplings of the tens of thousands of reports of near-death experiences begin to suggest this probability. As in life, there are some common experiences, in general, but there are also polar opposites and variations on themes and cultural influences that color the interpretation of the experience.

Maybe that's why our culture is beginning to respect people whose bodies or minds or senses aren't like everyone else's, because whose is? And maybe, just as there's no way to predict or determine what anyone else will experience in his or her body, there isn't any way to determine what someone will experience when he or she leaves this body. Maybe even that is a matter of personal choice. Our world religions have tour books and maps to give us some general idea of the territory that lies beyond our physical senses, but some of us have been noticing that a map isn't a whole lot like the actual landscape. Even though there are roads and universities and airports marked on the printout, the cliffs are unexpectedly stunning and the rivers aren't anything like their names and the wildlife wasn't even mentioned. Maybe how we live and how long we live and how we die and what we die into is simply up to each one of us.

If we knew that, of course, we'd have no need to impose our beliefs, or even our knowings, onto anyone else.

We could group together because we wanted to, not because we were afraid not to, although, if we were afraid not to, we could.

We could dare to be different, not because we resisted being part of a group, but because we decided to be part of a larger group or a smaller one, the smallest being one, as is the largest.

So, my Grander Self, have You anything to add to the discussion?

Snowflakes make snow.

What?

Can't have snow without snowflakes, can't find a snowflake like any other.

You're not feeling particularly brilliant this evening, are you?

On the contrary, I'm enjoying your brilliance, and it takes brilliance to know brilliance.

Oh. Why thank you. What an amazingly stupendous creation this multiverse is.

Why, thank you, I made it myself. And I couldn't have done it without you. And you, and him, and her, and it, and those, and them.

So we really are all in this together?

All.

Whether we're here for a fraction of a second or a million trillion years, we're all in this together.

I find that a very comforting thought. Don't you?

You do? You need us?

No snow without the snowflakes.

17

Draggin' in Our Myths

Since I'd had a manuscript accepted for publication, I'd become a little cocky. I didn't know this right away. All I knew was that I'd joined the ranks: I was a writer. And as a writer, I'd started reading about writing, and I came across a familiar but odd term, and I thought, no other profession that I know of takes such a perverse pride in what looks to me like a denial. You never hear about doctor's block or ballet dancer's block. Whenever I encountered someone discussing writer's block as if it were a foreseeable tragedy that must sooner or later be dealt with, my needle would jump into the danger zone. Uh-oh, red alert, new authors are being lured into the quicksand of cultural myths, quick, throw out a lifeline! Someone is saying, "Oh, you have writer's block, I've been there, let me tell you what to do about it," and I'm hearing, "Oh, you've exhaled every last ounce of your breath, let me tell you what to do next."

Writing, or creating, in whatever form we choose to create, creating our lives, I shrugged to myself, is a natural function of being alive, right? It's like eating when you're hungry, like breathing or eliminating or reproducing. It comes when it comes. It signals its presence. It can be put off for a while, but not for too long, and it can be coaxed to happen, but not forced.

Writer's block made me think of bulimia. A problem is created by a self-imposed restriction -- a certain allowable intake, a certain forced output -- and this self-imposed restriction comes from believing in a myth. I'm not thin enough. I'm not writing enough. I'm not good enough.

The reality behind the myth is, there's something here that I don't like.

If you liked your food, your body, your situation, you wouldn't be throwing up, and if you liked what you were writing, or creating out of your life, you would like getting back to it as soon as you could. It wouldn't be, oh no, I have writer's block, it would be, oh, I need to reproduce, or oh, I need to rest, or oh, I don't want to work for someone else for the rest of my life, which is partly why I became a writer, only obviously I am working for someone else, because if I were working for myself, I'd have a great boss who would understand words like inspiration and flow and three-week vacations.

Bulimia can be traced to a crisis of *I can't stomach any more of this.* It doesn't automatically come with the territory of having a stomach. Writer's block doesn't automatically come with the territory of being a writer. Getting stumped in creating the best possible life for oneself doesn't automatically come with the territory of being alive.

I might not know what I'm talking about. I've never had writer's block. Starting my writing as a fifteen-year-old girl being faithful to her diary and not writing anything publishable until the age of 55 disqualifies me from even saying the words *writer's block.*

But I do know something about draggin' on a dragon.

The dragon, in Celtic mythology (according to Richard Leviton in his provocatively multi-dimensional book *Looking for Arthur*), represents the human power of emotion, passion, turbulence -- chaotic and uncontrolled free will. A dragon-slayer, then, metaphorically speaking, is one who has transformed the unmanageable beast within, has used the sword of insight to master this truly pure form of energy.

Never having informed myself of the symbolism behind Arthurian imagery, I was mildly stunned to read in someone else's book a description of what had happened to me a dozen years before.

Someone close to me had attempted suicide. When I emerged from the hospital and from the numbing shock of how clueless I had been, a variety of emotions surfaced, self-blame, fear, grief, sorrow, compassion, anger at not having been given more signals so I could have helped sooner -- a whole jumble of emotions, but the one that kept rearing its ugly head the most was rage. Very ugly head. Dragon head. Baring its fangs, breathing fire, piercing the darkness with glowing red eyes. I kept shoving it back down my throat. I wanted to feel something, but this was very definitely not what I wanted to be feeling, not good enough, not even close, this dragon, this rage, rage at whom, rage at what? It wouldn't stay down. It kept rising from my depths, darting its evil eyes from side to side looking for something to scorch into annihilation.

Finally, lying on my bed that night, exhausted, I could no longer hold it back. I gave up. I unclenched my fists and let it go, terrified by what it might do. With my eyes closed, I watched the dragon fly off into the night, surrendering to whatever havoc it would wreak. Then, ruing my lack of control, I wanted to renege, drag it back, because of where it was landing. Arching its windblown-umbrella wings, the dragon descended over someone huddled in the corner of a dimly lit room, the person who had attempted suicide, crouching with knees drawn to chest, head hidden under folded arms. *No*, I screamed silently, at first at the dragon, but then, realizing the futility, at myself, no, you cannot stop it, face what your rage is doing, face it!

Why, why is my rage aiming for this person?

Hopelessly yielding, feeling as if I were being forced to view my own child being ravaged, I watched the dragon drop, its talons extended, its shadow looming over the despondent figure, who was unconscious of its presence. It landed silently. And then... it turned around, twisting its long scaly neck, lowering its snout, baring its fangs, and hissed fire out at the world, fuming flames of warning toward anyone who would harm this vulnerable, wounded person. No one would dare challenge such ferocity of purpose. The dragon had arisen to keep this person safe from a hurtful world.

Tears streamed from my eyes. I'd had no idea that I was so enraged at the *world* for being a place where any human being could be reduced to seeking self-destruction. I'd had no idea that within me was an archetypal creature, not of uncontrollable bestial passion and power, though it might have turned on me or become uncontrollable had I not given it its freedom, but of divine accordance with universal law.

I was, by Leviton's definition, a dragon-slayer, one who had transformed an unmanageable emotion into purity of intent, and my sword was the insight gained by surrendering a judging, controlling ego.

Dragon-slayer makes it sound somewhat ivory towers and damsels in distress, but the *myth* of the dragon -- that it is to be feared and slain – seems to me to be the same as the myth of the writer's block. The truth is, as Neale Donald Walsch's version of God says, what you resist persists. Or as my version says, if you cage it, you'll enrage it; free its intent, and you'll see its intent.

So, having dealt with dragons, I assumed I was in a position to offer some advice. If you do come up against writer's block, or any block, put away the sledgehammer and get out the spectacles. Is it a pebble or a boulder? An immovable mountain or an open-sesame slab of stone? Does it have any cracks? Are there any symbols engraved in it? What's on the other side of it? Oops. No fair peeking! Because once you do, you know, check to see what's on the other side, why, you're on the other side. It's no longer blocking your way.

I was quite proud of myself for having come up with this sound advice. I had no idea that the advice was meant for me.

Until my first book-length manuscript was returned to me.

Already? They've worked on it already? It has undergone its initial phase of editing, and I am to approve, revise, and return it to my editor as soon as possible. Does this mean it's coming out even sooner than I'd hoped? Oh, life is good, I crowed.

By the next morning, I was a wreck. I yelled at my family. If they ever let the dog out to bark at such an ungodly hour again, I was going to scatter poison all over the yard!

Remorse got the better of me to come out and apologize.

Then I went back inside and examined this slab of surliness between me and my good sense. It wasn't too hard to trace its inception to the arrival of my manuscript.

Life is good, I'd crowed. I have survived! I have survived the cavernous chasms that opened beneath me with every rejection! I have kept my footing atop the dizzying, upward-thrusting peak upon which is staked a victorious banner announcing publication! I have even survived an endless plateau of waiting, waiting for this final polish, a touch-up here, a blowing away of a little speck there.

I tossed the package onto my desk. I'm cool. There's no need to rush this. I'm calm. I don't need to open it just yet. I'm collected. I can putter and clean and watch TV. It's not as if the perfection of this book is the one defining deed upon which hinges the rest of my life. It's not as if I've envisioned a thousand dreams based on the income from this book, a house by the sea, lavish gifts for loved ones, trips to Borneo.

Or imagined the millions of people who will gasp and be instantly enlightened by the visible glow of its pages. Or reveled in the way so many readers' kindred minds will delight in a clever phrase here, an emerald necklace of lovely words there. I haven't seen myself interviewed by Oprah.

Well, okay, so maybe I have. So maybe I've been getting a little ahead of myself. So what does my editor think needs correcting?

No, not yet. Tomorrow. No need to be hasty. This is just another mundane chore, something I can tend to after a good night's sleep.

I turned out the light. Several sleepless hours later, at one in the morning, the dog reminded me that I forgot to let him inside. Not that he wanted to be let in. He was quite content to be outside, baying at the moon. I listened to those soaring howls and the neighborhood dogs' responses, a concert as soothing as a convoy of fire trucks, and I knew it was time to face the music.

Nevertheless, after getting Bo inside, I crawled back under my covers. My unopened, edited manuscript, however, was in the room with me, glowing green, a chunk of kryptonite, visible through my very eyelids and threatening to sap me of my sanity.

The dark hours between two and five began with a crooked smile of feeble self-reassurance. All those little yellow stickum notes, sprouting like so many mushrooms from the ragged right edge of what was once a crisp, clean presentation of my soul to the publisher, all those quickly scanned slashes and carets and ovals and arrows, those are not coffee grounds splattered onto a hopeless mess tossed into the garbage and then, oops, retrieved, to be returned to an unsuspecting first-time author. Those are acts of kindness. Say it again, with calm and control. Those are the efforts for which every author I've ever read has offered undying gratitude.

Okay. I take a deep breath, open to the first page, and look at the first correction. Oh, okay, I see that. Yeah, I can live with that.

We are going to be able to be mature about this, I tell myself with a hint of pride and relief, a little prematurely, for my reaction to the second correction is *What*? How can you eliminate this word? This word took me ten hours to hone in on! This word is the crux of the meaning of the entire half of this sentence! Are you some kind of illiterate idiot? (My editor, by the way, the "you" with whom I am now having an unmentionable conversation, has published his own staggeringly well-written books and probably has an IQ of 400.)

Well, I can see that I'm going to have to get myself a pad of little *blue* stickum notes, I decide as I move on to the third correction. I mean, I put that hyphen there for a reason. I intended that hyphen. That hyphen shifts the meaning of that phrase from one side of the universe to the other. This is absurd. Letting someone else tamper with the work of a genius. Would someone be allowed to eliminate an eyelash from the Mona Lisa? This is graffiti on the statue of David! Where did this guy learn his manners?

I look at the two chapters that he suggests need a bit of reworking. I sigh. He's right. They're awful. God, they're absolutely pathetic. Did I write these? What was I thinking? They should be eliminated entirely. Of course, that would cripple the flow of the book, but really, is this book worth saving? It's so unoriginal. (Never mind that when it first poured from my fingertips it made me laugh and cry and bounce on my office chair. I wrote this book a year ago, I reread it a hundred and seventy-two times, and there isn't a fresh word in it.) I flip the pages and come across a stickum note that convinces me I'm right, the book should be burned. It says, "I think this is one of your best chapters."

No, it isn't me who's convinced, it's a shriveled up little black fungus thing that is embedded in some corner of my innards. It snivels cloying phrases into my inner ear, like, "He likes one of your chapters and wants to toss two. Add it up, bimbo. Minus one. Your book is a negative quantity." This mosquito-whine drowns out whatever voice might have wanted to point out that there are forty-two other chapters with nothing but technical corrections. The fact that I've signed a contract and been given an advance is not even under consideration here. It's four in the morning and I have to rewrite two chapters by five. My editor wants my manuscript back in two weeks, but black fungus thing feeds on squeezing the trigger of my perfection-or-panic machine gun. If I don't come up with brilliance beyond compare before sunrise, I'll be so shot full of holes they'll have nothing to bury but tatters.

Rejection letters and acceptance calls are part of a landscape, topographical upheavals, events that happen out there. They have not prepared me for this at all. This editing business, this is inside my skin. Someone has ripped through the layers of my epidermis, of which I've been rather fond, as a whole, and is rearranging my organs, without an anaesthetic, and I am expected to smile appreciatively?

At sunrise, after an hour of sleep, the dog was outside, barking, and I was tempted to commit an atrocity.

But an examination of my resistance freed the truth. I'm going to be published! Someone cared enough to read every single word, to catch my mistakes, to clarify confusion, to suggest improvement, and to leave, look at it, ninety percent of the manuscript untouched, because, I must assume, it's good enough. Maybe not good enough to get me a televised meeting with Oprah, but really, would I want to subject myself to *that*? Make-up? Cameras? An audience of millions watching me spew spontaneous, unedited words from my lips? Better to be turned inside out, into a squirming, unidentifiable mass! Good enough to get published is good enough for me. I wanted to offer my undying gratitude to my editor, who, after all, wasn't cutting my heart out. He was just brushing the lint off my lapel.

I was content. I'd taken my advice.

Up to a point.

Up to the limit created by a myth.

A problem, a crisis, a kink in the natural flow is created by a self-imposed restriction that is based upon a myth. The myth is: I'm not good enough. The reality is that there's something I'm not embracing as good enough. There's something I'm not looking at as a valid and valuable part of my experience. There's something I'm not seeing for what else it could be.

Perhaps writer's block, or a block of any kind, is exactly what it looks like -- nothing more than a cause to pause. There's no reason not to pause, in the middle of an article on jellybeans, or in the middle of my life path, and share that I just ran smack into a wall of concrete and seriously damaged the wart on the end of my nose, but don't change the channel, we'll be right back, we've netted a big one, we're draggin' this myth into the lab, and if there's any life in it, we're reviving it, enlivening it, and elevating it to its rightful throne of truth.

We can always reconsider what to do about the pause, or the block, in the morning. That is, if it still exists. If it was real to begin with. If it wasn't just a dragon in our midst, much more well-intentioned than we knew -- offering us the opportunity to create our stories, and our lives, more closely from the core, with more of who we are, good enough to be and do whatever we desire.

18

Touch that Dial

Perceiving, or assembling the world into meaningfulness in particular ways, Don Juan told Carlos Castaneda, is accomplished from particular locations in the energy body. The usual position of the "assemblage point," the commonly rooted position that translates the world into its ordinary, mundane, rational appearance, is somewhere behind the right shoulder.

That didn't make much sense to me at the time when I had read it, years before, but then one day, as I sat quietly in my living room, I focused on that point. It seemed I knew exactly where it was. I took note of how I was perceiving the room. In an ordinary, rational way. There's a chair. There's the woodstove. Then, just by thinking that I could, I moved the assemblage point, which felt like a flattened sphere of reddish light energy about two inches in diameter, from behind my right shoulder over to somewhere behind my left shoulder, and as I did, even though my eyes were still reading objects, my perception shifted so noticeably that it seemed I'd just jolted my left side open with a tiny electric shock. Everything seemed transparent. All the objects I was looking at consisted of layers of motion. Atoms and molecules existed at their own rates of motion, or time, and the space between them at another. But what I was really excited about was what had happened when I moved the assemblage point. The sensation was that my energy body was a gridwork of lines of light – picture a computerized three-dimensional ovoid blueprint, circumscribed with slats of electric-blue light. When I shifted the flattened sphere from the right to the left, it didn't slide over the grid, it stayed attached to it, like a knob, and the entire gridwork was shifted, as if I'd just opened the air-conditioning vent in my car, all the little slats moving in sync. What I had been experiencing before, I could tell by the contrast of what I was experiencing now, had been a reception of information all over, not just through eyes and ears, but now there was a different slant, a polarized retake, of the information that was being received by the entire surface of my energy body. I had a spherical awareness of the spaciousness behind me, beneath me, of the energy levels and frequencies of everything around me, with no sense of up or down, of gravity or disconnectedness.

I shifted the point of awareness back to my right shoulder, and the grid slid with it, closing off the 360-degree x-ray vision as if I'd turned the rod on the window blinds. Wow, cool, I thought. I sat there like a kid, sliding myself open and shut, as if I'd just learned how to wink both eyes, one at a time, to make my raised finger move back and forth without moving it.

Then it occurred to me that I could slide my energy grid into yet another position. So, with a thought, I slid the knob to the top of my head. Whoa. Roller coaster upside-down swirl, but then, whee, I was out, my eyes closed themselves off from seeing the room and I was out of my body, flying somersaults over my own head, zooming up and diving and spiraling into a multidimensional dance of freedom.

Okay, that was fun, slide the knob back to the right shoulder blade and catch my breath.

This kind of discovery makes me feel like an infant discovering that my arms are attached to me. It's very much like that. I still don't know how I move my arm. I just use a glance to let it know where I want it to go, and it goes there. I don't have to use a glance, though, I can use a mental image. And I can use no image at all. I can just desire that my arm reach out, and it does. And even if I don't have any desires or thoughts at all, my arm will just reach up and wave back when someone waves at me!

This is magic!

I took a walk that evening and noticed that my little knob of perception was somewhere behind my right shoulder, and everything looked normal, the trees fluttering their autumn-colored leaves in the cool breeze, the tall paper-dry corn plants in long rows, the clusters of

Queen Anne's Lace, the long-needled pines beyond, all was the same landscape through which I had taken evening walks for years.

Then, the same way that I move my arm, by magic, I shifted my sphere of perception over to behind my left shoulder, and instantly I sensed the immensity of the planet, the vastness of space beneath, behind, and all around me, the transparency of the trees and the fields, the dream-like energy of it all. I felt so sensitive to the subtleties of energy shifts that I was suddenly positive there was something alive and mobile just past the last row of corn. I took a few more soft-shoed steps, and two startled fawns bolted across the alfalfa field, slowing to an easy bounce when they sensed my lack of interest. I wondered where their points of perception are in their energy bodies, and whether they can shift them. I suspect that if I were to exercise this position of perception, I might be able to answer such questions with direct awareness.

I walked on, and decided to move the knob into my heart.

I become the trees; they are me, loving myself as their rootless explorer self. The breeze is me, caressing myself. The planet is me, smiling beneath and behind it all. It is all the same loving presence, dressed in different colors, presenting different faces and textures out of a love of creating, creating differences, subtle ones, powerful ones, all the same, differences for the sake of having more to love.

I begin to understand.

So what happens when I move my point of perception into my root chakra, which has to do with material survival, groundedness, aggression and passion, self before tribe? What would happen for someone else, I'm sure, would be different from what happened for me. I was taken aback. With my point of perception located in my root chakra, I saw the trees as objects that I could use for my own ends -- in my case, objects that I wanted to paint. I wanted to possess them, objectify them, preserve them in my own way, for my own purposes. I was surprised at how aggressive that felt. (I was also rather relieved that I didn't have an irresistible desire to chop them down and turn them into other objects that I could use or sell.) My perception was most definitely in terms of things that I could make use of for my own survival. My awareness of the different shades of color had to do with greed and was accompanied by a sub-human growl of pleasure. I wanted to capture the colors, manipulate them, apply my own intentions to them. I wanted to make the colors mine and sell them. The word enslave comes to mind. I understood a way of perceiving that permeates materialistic and imperialistic societies as I never had before.

This was about the extent of my attention span for the evening, but it gave me plenty to think about. It's a little like the story of the six blind men and the elephant. It's also, like, man, our human cultures argue over who is right about what color the grass is on the other side of the fence and we don't even notice that we're all wearing different- colored sunglasses. It's like being an infant, too, who doesn't get it yet, that's my fist holding that blanket. Oh! You mean I will also be able to pick up a rattle, turn myself over, *walk* like they do?

How come nobody ever told me I could do this?

You have been told that you can do this, and you have been doing this.

Yeah, that's the other thing. I was going to say that. I've *been* doing it. I just didn't know what I was doing. This is another kind of freedom, another kind of fluidity. What we think of as normal percep... by the way, who was that talking to me just now?

That was what happens to your perception when you move that knob to yet another point on or within your energy body. You have an unlimited number of points of perception.

I don't think I would have understood that remark quite the way I do right now, without having just taken that walk. But I was probably getting a very low impact reception of what is possible to receive.

Yes, you were. What is possible to perceive is the sensation of having changed the dream scene, having shifted the reality entirely, having created another world. But you don't need to worry about that just yet. Just get the hang of what you're doing now, and each new skill will follow. All humans will eventually recognize themselves as beings of infinite flexibility, if they so desire. You are one of many assisting the greater mindset to adjust to this potential. There are many realities. We cannot tell you in ways that you can understand as yet, but you can, truly, with the freedom you are developing, change your experiences, and experience your changes, as painlessly and effortlessly as you do when you raise your arm and wave.

So you're available to me because I've shifted my little knob?

You could call it your point of referral.

Oh.

Or your translator. Or your polarized magnifying glass. Information can be translated for you and by you from the energy matrix — which is not the same as portrayed in the movie The Matrix, *by the way, although that movie was making an excellent point about the general belief system concerning reality. All interpretations have their validity. It is impossible to translate the Ultimate Reality into any system of communication that is less than the entire ongoing self-creating experience. The purpose of the experience includes interpretations, as it includes awareness of the miracle and mystery of itself. Your interpretations are your stories, as are those of every aware being, and they color, transmute, augment, and enhance the One Story. You have the choice of interpretation as well as of creation of your contribution to the Story.*

I can just touch that dial! Use my imagination as one of my extra senses. Know that I am a miracle. Bask in the miraculous.

The miraculous is simply that which is not yet understood or experienced as part of the All that you are.

Thank you.

You are welcome. It is with infinite devotion that we depart.

You sound familiar.

You have heard from us before.

And I will again?

As you will, so shall it be.

19

If the Shoe Fits

I am a loser. I am losing it. I am at a loss.

This is a temporary state. It can change. It will change. At the moment, I can't do a thing to rearrange my external circumstances, any more than I could propel being six months pregnant into being delivered. But I can foresee deliverance.

Right?

Wrong.

Daily sighs, doses of why bother to go on, that sort of thing. So I pick up a book and open it, and I am told, *if the shoe fits, the foot is forgotten*.

Hah.

The point seems to be that if the shoe doesn't fit, you're *supposed* to notice, and, *duh*, take it off. Which is what some part of me seems to be trying to do. It's been noticing that something isn't right, and it's been squirming by night and grumping by day, while this other part of me keeps saying I must be losing it, and keeps trying to hold on to whatever it is, this shoe, when the obvious solution is to get out of it, get it lost, be losing it, be emptying out, breathing out, barefoot, naked.

How can I so easily forget these cycles, living on this revolving planet as I do?

Going through a change of heart shouldn't have to be any more traumatic than watching a sunset. Feeling uninspired and unmotivated and purposeless shouldn't be any more upsetting than putting on my pajamas.

Sometimes I forget that I am just a tourist, visiting this revolving planet from a place of no dichotomy at all. It is easy to forget, with the sun at just that distance, with the moon alone at night. I seem to remember, somewhere in my imagination, a larger sun glowing rosily, a father beaming warmth to a babe in arms, and right behind it, smiling too, another sun, who moves into the foreground in a dependable rotation of appearance. This sun, our Sol, who stands apart, who disappears behind the gray of cloud for days, seems less involved, as if to insist into our psyches that we are here to grow up on our own, become our own inner suns and daughters. And the moon, this moon, what does she tell us, all alone at night? I remember many moons, cavorting across each other's orbits, grouping now and then, or strung out in playful rows, all different sizes and colors. A family of moons, none of which would ever know the loneliness of an only child. I forget that this single planet, this isolated child of a single parent, this single parent of an only moon, finds itself sighing, worried, challenged, pleading, perhaps as often as it takes comfort in the closeness of its little inhabitants. But it could be lonely. For that matter, it could be seriously emotionally disturbed.

Fires are raging across the western states. My sister's eyes are burning and she can't see the mountains from her house because of the gray haze -- and she lives 150 miles from the source of the smoke. I can't remember this soggy an August in Pennsylvania. Every night another thunderstorm grumbles and crackles and sends waves of windswept rain across the countryside. Every afternoon it happens again. The plants are loving it, the corn is ten feet tall, but I expect to see people tubing by on my whitewater driveway any minute now. Mother Nature is restless. I'm feeling the same way. Smoke is getting in my eyes. I'm crying waves.

What's going on in here? There seem to be an awful lot of little selves split into fragments inside me, and you guys don't seem to be getting along very well. Come on, folks, somebody tell me what's wrong. What is that smoke in there?

That smoke is a screen, and I appear to be the spokesman here, and I'm telling you, these wimps in here just don't know how to tough it out, is all.

Oh. What are we toughing out?

We are obviously moaning and groaning with self-pity when there's everything to be grateful for. We have elected ourselves to be harbingers of good news, and we're falling down on the job here.

Well, maybe you're being a little hard on somebody. Does anybody else have anything to say about this?

I want out. Just let me out. I want to move. Pack up and go. To the ocean. To the future. To the stars. To anywhere but here.

See that? We've got an escapist in our midst. Shape up! You really think somewhere else is going to be better than here? You want to go be alone somewhere?

No. Alone is scary.

Hey, you can do alone, woman. You've done alone. You're tough. Don't let fear stop you from finding your true destiny.

Destiny schmestiny. I don't need a destiny. I need somebody to care about how I'm feeling. Nobody cares. Nobody cares that I have been crying my eyes out for days now.

Well, you don't tell anybody. You hide it. You go off. What do you expect? See, this is what I don't like. I'm trying to get you to remember to create your own life, and you're falling apart...

Shush now. Humbling, that's what you are afraid of, my little toughie, of finding out how small you are, how much you need others to help you feel okay about life. And let me tell you, it's understandable, you're afraid to need, you're afraid to ask, you have toughed it out, and I'm grateful to you, even though you get hard and cold and remote sometimes, I know you love this inner family. I just want to reassure you all that it's okay to want to run away, and it's okay to cry, and it's okay to feel small and helpless.

Why, because everything will change? We're aging and will fall apart even more, but someday we'll die and get eaten by worms? Life is basically a no-win situation and who in the universe talked us into coming here to this planet anyway?

Maybe when it's raining this much, for this many weeks, you might as well just go right out into it and get sopping wet, drenched, plastered to your own skin, and cry out to the gods, "What's going on?"

I did that once, about sixteen years ago. I was caught in such an unresolvable dilemma that I went out into the middle of a storm and yelled at the universe. Two rather amazing things happened.

Oh, yeah?

This conversation with myself is getting absurd. I'm pretending I don't remember what happened and I want to hear the story?

Oh, get a grip and tell us what happened.

Well, I took a look at myself from the outside. When you're doing something that looks a little too much like a scene in a movie, like shaking your fist at a thunderstorm that's drenching you with truckloads of pelting rain, it's easier to slip into the audience, and either notice what an idiot you're being, or give up and watch the movie.

The second thing that happened, though, that was something else. The storm talked back. I yelled out a question. A bolt of lightning crackled and shuddered and boomed right over my head.

I lowered my fist. "Are you talking to me?" I asked.

I got a rumble in response.

"Let me get this straight," I said. And no matter how long it took me to pose my question, Mother Nature waited until I was finished, and then gave me what felt like a totally appropriate powerful Yes or a subdued Hmm or a grumbling Think about it, kid. By the time our conversation was finished, I knew more than I had before. I was soaked, cleansed, and lucid.

The next day, what we had talked about was confirmed.

I was at the Jersey shore. It was midnight, and I had just popped awake at the sound of someone calling my name. No one was there. I got up and slipped out of the motel room, passed a group of partiers on the balcony on my way to the stairs, and went down to the beach. Beyond the light of the motel, I stood on the cool sand, facing the moonlit waves, and implored Nature again, the moon, the sea, the wind, the stars in the darkened sky, to converse with me, to tell me what to do. Although I couldn't hear anything over the rushing of the waves as they tumbled around my bare feet, I sensed someone approaching. I wrapped my arms around my nightie and turned around.

"Are you okay?" A young man in his twenties, one of the people partying on the balcony, had followed me from the motel.

"I was just asking the universe to give me love and understanding," I said, not thinking until the words were out of my mouth that I must look and sound like an escapee from the nuthouse.

"I thought you might be doing something like that," he said gently, nodding. "I followed you because I have this, uh, guardian angel feeling toward you." He shrugged. "I think God sent me to you."

I cocked my head at him. I wasn't much into the word "God" at the time. God was somebody the evangelists on TV were selling to desperados.

He proceeded to give me, in the course of a casual conversation, several messages, the most pertinent of which, at the time, was, "Share the control." He couldn't have known how applicable that statement was to my predicament, but then, he didn't have to, he was just some good-hearted guy making sure some weird forty-year-old woman was okay.

Neither did he know that a few weeks earlier I had gone into a meditation, during which I found myself entering a chamber beneath a huge pyramid. In the middle of the chamber was a golden sphere perched on a pedestal, and on the sphere was the indentation of two handprints. I had slipped my hands into the indentations, a perfect fit, and had been inundated with cosmic information.

A lot of good that was doing me now.

"I read in the paper recently," he said, standing beside me and looking out at the crests of the dark waves lit by the light from the motel, "that they found a crystal sphere off the coast of Bermuda. Under the water, inside a pyramid. It was sitting on a pedestal, and it had two golden hands attached to it. When they moved it, the whole world shifted. In a way that people don't know about yet."

My face fell open. I stared at him. I wasn't sure whether the light I noticed around him was a halo or the glow from Atlantic City several miles to the north. It didn't occur to me to ask him what paper. I didn't care. I was feeling the world shift. Never having considered what blurted out of my mouth next, I was surprised to hear myself say, "I have the feeling we knew each other in Atlantis."

He turned to me. "Of course we did."

He wasn't smiling. Suddenly I wanted to laugh. But then, laughing in the face of God, it seemed, might be a little shabby on my part. Well, okay, I wasn't quite ready yet to call it God, but maybe this was another way that the universe carried on a conversation, and maybe I'd better listen.

"I also read that extraterrestrial beings are going to manifest themselves to us, for the purpose of teaching us."

Whoa. Are we talking aliens? "When is this supposed to happen?" I asked, having trouble hiding a smile, not noticing the subtle differences between the words *aliens* and *extraterrestrials*.

"Within our lifetimes," he said.

And then he proceeded to tell me that when I got home, if I had any more questions, I should let the Bible fall open, and where my eyes fell, I would find my answer.

I did that, I sat with the Bible in my hand a few days later and asked, what was that all about? The words that jumped up off the page at me were, "And God sent his angel to show the way." I cried.

It took a few months for the dilemma to unravel, which it did when I shared the control.

The storm knew what it was talking about when it told me I was being heard, and answered. There are always answers.

If the shoe doesn't fit, I can jump up and down and throw a tantrum, and notice what an idiot I'm being, or I can just sit down and untie the laces and slip it off.

Aaaah. That feels better.

Ooh, I could get into this! Never wearing shoes at all, ever again! Well, until I want to go somewhere or do something that requires shoes, and then, well, a shoe or two that fits would be in order.

My grandson Eli's Waldorf School teacher took his mother, my step-daughter Raine, aside and told her that an evaluation was needed to assess how to help her son overcome his evident difficulty with math. Raine was concerned enough about what Eli would have to go through to remark to me, sadly, that she wished everything could be easy for her son. Although neither of us are the type to shirk a challenge, her comment triggered some deep response in me about old paradigms. I looked back, not too many years ago in our history, at lefties being smacked on their hands until they gave up their natural inclination in favor of an imposed superstition. Fortunately, children no longer have to sit in corners wearing dunce caps – they are prescribed glasses or remedial classes. People who can't use their legs are given wheelchairs and ramps. Adults who can't add fast enough use calculators. But there is still some outdated supposition governing most of the western institution of education that all students must conform to a standard of mathematical proficiency. Fourth-graders are not evaluated for how to overcome colorblindness. If they're colorblind, well, shrug, that's that. If they can't *add*, well, there goes half the SAT score and the whole of their future, not to mention the future of their country.

I remember my daughter Fawni crying over math problems. When she could have been given a calculator. Because there is no reason why things can't be easy for our children -- and for all of us who are presumed to be handicapped or less proficient or challenged in some area or another, which is absolutely everybody I know, most of all *me*. We don't all wear size seven brown leather loafers. Some of us can't do the same thing for forty-seven years, or even for two. Some of us can't balance a checkbook without counting on our fingers, or cope with our youngest leaving the nest without falling apart and hearing voices.

Fortunately, the Waldorf system of education encourages a conscious approach to difficulties. The entire staff began to meditate and pray on Eli's behalf, directing love and guidance toward him and asking for an inspired solution. Since the shoe didn't fit, the approach used in class, arrangements were made for Eli to be tutored by a patient and appreciative teacher. Within a few weeks, he was getting better at math. He was almost enjoying it. He had needed a different pair of shoes, and the people responsible for his comfort complied with his needs.

I've been grumping because I've internalized a standard, because I still judge myself for my differences, my growth spurts, my slow periods, my natural cycles, because someone by the name of Lesta promoted being joyful when that was how she felt and someone else by the name of Lesta is expecting that Lesta to remain constant and this Lesta is a loser.

This is scary stuff, this figuring out how to live happily ever after, one day at a time. I've thought I stepped out of the maze before. Wow. Freedom. Open horizons. Great view. Breathtaking. So breathtaking I can't breathe. Maybe I better step back, just lean against this wall, and catch my breath. Oh, what's that, someone behind me is calling. Maybe I should turn around and help him find his way out. I don't want to leave anyone behind, this is too great, this view, way too great, I don't think I can look at it alone, why don't I just go back in there and take this turn, no wait, turn here, where, where are you, wasn't someone calling me? Uh oh. Help!

I'm standing on the threshold again, swearing I will never go back into that maze. I am the Tarot Fool, stepping into the unknown, after having expanded through the cycle all the way to this one level of mastery. This is what comes next, knowing next to nothing.

But this could be okay. It's as if I've broken out of a contained sphere of experience that took me a while to explore to its fullest, a sphere that finally became too cramped. This being thrust out into the next larger sphere is scary and disorienting, it's bigger than I can see the end of, I'm just opening my eyes to it, it's going to take a while to get my bearings. I've lost the security of the smaller sphere, and I'm flailing... but I could be floating, I could just relax, I might just notice that I'm not sinking or shrinking after all, I'm... I'm growing? Oh! Of course the shoe no longer fits. I'm growing!

This loser who is losing it appears to be lost in a sea of nothing to lose. There appears to be no me. Nobody here but a flake, melting on God's tongue.

20

Only Children

China, until not too long ago, was a nation of only children. I've read that when the children were brought together into groups, some of them were shy, some resisted compromising, and some were so refreshed, so eager for relationship, that they cried when they had to leave. China is a sizable chunk of humanity, a significantly large portion of our species' global body, experiencing the solitude, the over-indulgence, the special self-awareness of an only child. If we do not remember from where else we came, if we do not embrace our origins, all the other places in the universe we have known and loved within the multiverse, if we confine ourselves to Earth with a one-child-family attitude, what will we become? Perhaps China is going to show us that. Perhaps she will mirror something to the rest of us that will teach us something we need to know. Perhaps her boundaries will have to split, or soften, and she'll pour herself into the rest of us, resisted or accepted, a disease or a healing, a part of this evolution that is shaking all of us to ask ourselves, what are we becoming? What can we become?

I posed those questions to myself, only to have them answered as soon as I emptied out all my resistance to the change experienced by an empty-nester and headed west to visit my daughter.

China's only children were, at the time I was thinking about them, already in their early twenties. I didn't know this until my sister invited my traveling companion, Mary, and me to a friend's apartment for dinner. Seven of us, four middle-aged American women and three

113

Chinese grad students working toward their masters' in various sciences at Montana State, sat around the small table on a haphazard assortment of chairs enjoying real Chinese food and exchanging cultural points of view.

The young man and one young woman are both only children. One of them said he wished he'd had brothers and sisters, and the other said she was happy to be an only child. The other young woman, who has an older sister, said she'd often wished she were an only child. As they updated us on the one-child-per-family legislation being amended to two and verbalized the pros and cons of their own experiences, I began to understand that there is no way to generalize what China is like, no matter how many children there are. Just like anywhere else on the planet, despite the cultural overlay, every single person has his or her own set of assumptions, emotions, challenges, and advantages.

In the excitement of exchange, the mutually polite attentiveness melted into eager questions and answers, and then into teasing and laughing, punctuated with groans of pleasure over the delicious meal. All seven of us, by the time we parted, had had a thoroughly delightful evening.

I awoke the next morning from a dream in which we were all sitting around the same table talking, just as we had been. In the dream I suddenly remembered having worked on a peace quilt. Oh, yes, so did the person sitting next to me remember working on a peace quilt. The next person, too, knew what we were talking about. It turned out that each of us had worked on the peace quilt, which was traveling around the world, being added to piece by piece, by everyone into whose hands it came.

When I shared the dream with Mary and Celia, we decided to start an actual peace quilt, one that we would pass on to our new Chinese friends. Mary and I liked the idea so much that we began several more and left them with various people as we traveled around the country. As I stitched a trapezoid of green and purple flowers onto the spiraling patchwork, a sense of peace pervaded me, a sense of comfort, at the thought of this quilt passing through many creative, loving hands before ending up with some homeless person or underprivileged child. Wouldn't it be wonderful, I thought, if people who had added to this quilt decided to start others, and if peace quilts were being worked on all around the world, to be accepted by whoever needed them when they were finished? Each person who slept beneath a peace quilt would feel warmed by the love of so many unknown benefactors.

We decided to label the center circle of each one that we started with its own date and place of origin. Someday someone in China, perhaps, or who knows where, will wrap himself up in a randomly colorful quilt that was begun in Bozeman, Montana, in September of 2000. Maybe he will have heard the story, that it was started because of a dream, or maybe the story, whispered down the lane, will have taken on a new meaning with each passing of the quilt into willing, agile hands.

Let there be peace on earth, goes the song sung at the end of a Unity gathering, and let it begin with me.

Let us focus into this, our arena of questions, conflicts, and fears, our little sphere of experience in the sky, and bring our compassion, our loving and sagacious warmth, our generosity and peaceful joy into this world. We can do this. I can rethink myself into joy, and radiate it outward from this inner sun that I was taught to shape inside my earthling form, from this inner daughter grown into a crone. You can rethink yourself into peace, despite the conflict, or perhaps because of it, because it is urging you to become a ray of light.

You picked up this book because you wanted to remember. I am telling you all this because I wanted to remember. Beyond and within a frame of time, you and I are sharing open hearts and minds and souls, loving our fragile planet even while we are intimidated by her power, just as much as we are loving our own fragile selves, and are intimidated by our own power.

Of course we are. You wouldn't be reading this if you were completely at home with your power. I wouldn't be writing it.

We are only children, after all.

And we're so much more. We are the beauty of this mysterious little corner of the galaxy, this singleness that reaches toward togetherness, bursting with curiosity, expanding into infinite possibilities, embracing an eternity of unfolding events.

Thank you for being in my future, for holding this book in your hands in your present, for reaching back through time and giving me a reason to offer my thoughts. By the way, what's it like there in that future? Has anyone invented ways to replace fossil fuels with water and sunlight? Oh, wait, that's already happening. Has anyone started the development of a Department of Peace in our government? Oh, wait, that's already happening, too. Has China been softening its boundaries? Oh, wait, yes, that, too. Is there a global network of communication? Ah, yes. Is there a different attitude about war and poverty and disease?

For a world of only children, we're doing some rather mature and masterful manifesting of the best possible realities.

21

Out of the Box

A friend's comments about her cubicle work space — she was feeling closed in, but after all, it was a good-paying job — maybe she'd get a potted plant — and she did have all the health benefits she could possibly want — reminded me of the one joke I've been able to retain in that miniscule part of my brain allotted to joke retention.

The new cowpoke on a cattle drive sat with the other cowboys around their first night's campfire and hungrily accepted a plate of beans and a tin mug of coffee. He sipped the coffee and nearly choked. This was the worst cup of coffee he had ever tasted. He gagged on the beans. How could anyone eat anything so foul? He watched in disbelief as the other men shoveled in their chow. What was wrong with them? He spat out his food. "This here's the worst durned excuse for vittles I ever come across." The other men hooted and guffawed. They had a rule they hadn't let him in on. Whoever complained about the food was going to have to be the next night's cook. Not particularly thrilled with having been the brunt of their humor, the greenhorn drove the chuck wagon the next day, stopping occasionally to collect condiments for the evening meal. As the cowboys sat around the campfire that night, the new cook passed out what looked like meat pies. With raised eyebrows, the men accepted the tasty-looking dishes and avidly shoveled forkfuls into their mouths. To the new cook's smug delight, their faces turned green as soon as they began to chew. One man managed to squeak,

"Why, this here's... *moose turd* pie!" He swallowed, with difficulty, and trying not to grimace, nodded his head slowly. "*Good*, though."

All the "health benefits" she could possibly want? What an interesting concept. Spending the better part of your life in a cubicle is not going to be alleviated by a potted plant, but if you will accept payment for boxing yourself into their regime even though it doesn't suit your nature, they'll pay for some of the inevitable damage and call it "health benefits."

My friend shared with the rest of us gathered that evening that she thought maybe she should be grateful for this job that is so much better than the last one she had. But she keeps finding herself slipping out of the box, she said, and it gets harder and harder to squeeze herself back in.

Another friend picked up on the phrase. As he watched the fiasco of recounting the votes in Florida to determine whether Gore or Bush would assume the presidency, he kept shaking his head at the proposed solutions to the problem. They're looking for answers inside the box, he said. The solutions can't be seen from inside the box.

Setting up metal detectors in high schools doesn't change the fact that there are teenagers who are violently unhappy with being boxed inside of concrete walls with frustrated, overworked teachers.

Suing an overworked and exhausted doctor for malpractice doesn't change the fact that someone ended up in a box that cost her family more than an outrageous amount of money.

People are eating fast food boxed lunches of moose turd pie and grinning crookedly as if they've outwitted somebody.

When someone approaches the witness box, he's asked, "Do you swear to tell the truth, the whole truth, and nothing but the truth, so help you God?" I'd like to hear a witness respond, "If all of you will swear to let me." And when he's cut off with, "Answer the question, yes or no," I'd like to hear him say, "But I swore to tell the whole truth." Okay, so what we've got is better than being intimidated by men in preposterous white wigs, but even with women judges, we're still acting from inside the box. Nevertheless, like the hybrid electric-gas car, the witness demanding that the whole truth be told would be a step toward the threshold. Having both undervalued teenagers and undervalued teachers contribute their needs and their visions to a discussion of possible changes within the existing educational system is a hybrid solution, too, a mere half-step toward removing the word *compulsory* from its partnership with education, as would be insisting on more time for doctors and patients to discuss the truth of their humanness, their limitations, and their expectations, on the way to both of them recognizing from whence cometh the healing. But half-steps are better than no steps.

Right? Well, to a point. No steps, no visible means of expansion within the given structure, could be part of a perfectly natural and divine timing. There comes a moment when the fetus is just too cramped, and if it doesn't just go ahead and break out of confinement, well, no more growth. It's either die inside what was once comfortable, or risk the unknown and expand into a greater potential. Humanity is experiencing serious labor pains, and we're scared. We just spent a metaphorical nine months bringing the seed of great potential to the brink of deliverance, and now we're wondering, what are all these wrenching implosions?

What are we about to give birth to? What do we have to go through to do so?

It strikes me as interesting that the book of Revelations describes a third of all living things being wiped out before humanity enters its golden age of a thousand years, and that the placenta, which accounts for about a third of the weight gain of pregnancy, is cast off at birth, having fulfilled its temporary purpose. How much of what was needed to get us where we are is no longer useful? What is it that has to be discarded during this breakthrough into a new reality? What kind of protective shielding, living structure, is it time to cut ourselves free from? Who or what comprises the container that has outlived its provision of security? Does it have to be so frightening, that something will die in the process of giving birth? Can we regard the box, the placenta, the overly complex and no longer effectively functional institutions -- of government, economics, religion, law, education, marriage, medicine -- with gratitude and finality as we gradually bid those current forms of social management farewell? Can we free ourselves into becoming a human family in which every member participates in the decisions that affect their lives by expressing their needs and their talents, in which every member contributes to and receives from our global abundance according to abilities and requirements, in which every member is regarded as another beloved facet of the whole, a teacher as well as a student, a unique individual as well as a cooperative partner, a self-healing soul as well as a healer?

In fact, people everywhere *are* stepping out of the box, and maybe that's the way it needs to happen, not by being told from the outside what to do, but to honor the driving impulses from within.

How hard can it be, if we don't resist when the time is right, to flow out of the cubicles, the boxes, the wombs, the outmoded ways of life, and into the unlimited horizons of new life?

Okay, hard, if we're still attached, and even if we don't resist, maybe still the hardest thing we'll ever do.

It's scary, the prospect of a new life in which we are no longer being fed through a tube but have to use our own mouths.

But if I focus on the fear, it's kind of like gaping in horror at the fuel gauge needle hitting the E and then slamming on the brakes in hopeless resignation. If I use the gauge as an indication of what I need to do next, and focus on what I need to do next, why then, I fuel up at the next gas station, or, in one possible future, refill the pollution-free hydrocell with water.

I recently read about a therapist who used hypnosis on her clients so they could focus on something that looked unnervingly fear-oriented to me. After having been surprised by what emerged from her first few patients, she began suggesting to subsequent patients – and this felt really creepy to me – that they too might have demons inside them causing their symptoms, entities separate from themselves. The patients would proceed to locate the demons, have conversations with them, and find out that the devil had instructed them to mess with the patients' heads and bodies. Then the patients, with the therapist's guidance, would tell the demons to see the spark of light deep within themselves, and to go into the Light. The demons would be reluctant, having been convinced that they would be tortured if they disobeyed instructions, but they would discover that the Light felt peaceful and loving, and they would turn around, say thank you, and then go into the Light. Time and again, the patients found themselves almost instantly relieved of their symptoms.

Then, because the demons had described the ease of entry into their victims being at its greatest during a lapse in physical health or emotional stability, the therapist gave her clients a prayer with which to strengthen their etheric bodies and to assure angelic protection so that they couldn't be invaded again. The patients reported continued health and well being.

I don't have a problem with regarding the forces of love as entities – angels, guardian spirits, God. So why am I uncomfortable with regarding the forces of evil as entities? I don't even like to say the word evil. I don't want to give it that much substance. I'd rather see it as an absence. But it could easily be assumed that there is more than an absence, there is some active energy, some force within and behind the insanity. What name it is given and how it is interpreted is a question of focus.

What this therapist was doing, apparently, was helping her clients focus, not on something fearful, but on the gauge needle pointing to a need for action. Whatever was causing the pain or the phobia or the disorder, whether it was self-created blocked energy, external pollution, missing soul parts, viral invasion, palpable negativity directed at them from someone else, leftover scars from a past life, or even a recruit of the devil, it was an alarm that indicated the need for action. It was time to look for that Light station in the sky.

Since I've found it helpful to accept the presence of angels, it could conceivably be as helpful to regard negative forces as demons with their own identities, for then they too can be addressed. In the bigger picture, angels and demons are the same as saints and stalkers, different facets of universal consciousness, different rates of motion, different frequencies in the grand spectrum of being. In this smaller picture, it's comforting to assume that there are loving ethereal entities in addition to inspired humans. And it's a challenge to understand the drive behind a power-hungry politician or a terrorist, let alone an invisible representative of Satan.

Ms. God, what were you thinking?

My dears, I think through you. My thoughts are vast, and yet when they come through you, and you, they become specific, and they create what is all around you and within you. You have thought this world into what it is. You have created these challenges, these puzzles, these beauties and these horrors. You have all the information and all the power you need to create whatever reality you intend to experience. You can see your collective selves as being born. Or you can see your race as having reached adolescence and being confused by all the information and power available to you. You can see humanity as being so uneasy, so diseased, that you are unable to reconnect to your original Self except by leaving the gravity of the matter you have created. Or you can regard your separate cultures and religions as having been separate seeds in need of protection and nurturing until the garden has sprouted a wide variety of foods that can now be shared by all. You can imagine and realize whatever you will.

This is scary, you know. That it's up to us. We are so far from perfect. I have made so many mistakes. I have hurt so many people with my thoughtlessness. I wasn't given enough by my parents to walk through life as a saint, but it isn't their fault, they weren't given enough by parents who were given even less. The chain rattles from so far back into misty time. How do I break it? How can I stop the chain from rattling into the lives of future generations? I've already failed my children in so many ways, ways that will be passed on to their children. I'm afraid it's already too late.

What you are fearing is feared by many. The perpetuation established within the pattern is as it seems, and yet there is a pattern beyond this pattern. Look at the tapestry of humanity. See the colors for what they are, dramatic splashes of color, woven threads that die out or turn into brilliant scenes. An artist's early works, though they haven't the mastery demonstrated in later ones, are nevertheless valued as the progressive development of themes and techniques.

Okay, so I can look at my mistakes as a learning process, but what can I do now about their repercussions on the lives of others?

Begin with self-forgiveness, which is nothing more than slipping out of the chains, out of the river, out of the very tapestry itself, to realign yourself with your ability to comprehend and recreate. Ask for what you want, a better life, a better world, and it will be yours. Do not let yourself be pulled backwards, inextricably linked to the misconceptions of the past. Recognize that you are not powerless. Break away from the fear of your own mastery. Bring joy and gratitude into your present by knowing and receiving what gives you pleasure, inspiration, and energy, and you will be able to see it all with love, and to love those behind, around, and ahead of you as they stumble and triumph through their own chosen dramas. Only on one level have you been the result of a chain reaction. This is a part of the third-and-fourth-dimensional reality, in which you experience the repercussions of past experiences as causing ensuing experiences. The chain reaction is a natural part of this dimension, as are ripples on a pond. Look through the surface. The disturbance beneath the surface is nothing but a shifting of the light. You are the ripples. And you are also the light.

The dissolving of the chains will open many heretofore unimagined avenues. Dissolve them by understanding that action creates reaction, that the links are hooked when you strain against or away from what you perceive as dark forces, undoable wrongs, evil outcomes. Relax and let the greater reality be what it is, and the chains are no longer needed to keep in or keep out. All becomes motion, fluidity, part of the warp and woof of creation.

We are more powerful than our past mistakes.

Indeed. In thought, in word, in action, in deed. You have the greatest powers in the universe right inside of you.

Love. And fear! Anger, and innocence. Consciousness, and ignorance. I have the power of ignorance inside me, if that's what I choose to use. I can be blissful in my ignorance. Or unhappy in it. I can be unhappy in my consciousness. Or happy. I can use the gift of happiness, and I can put it aside. I can stay awake, and yet sometimes I will want to sleep. I can change the world, as well as accept it as it is. I can feel alone, or I can know that I have a friend. And whether we call our friend Michael or God or You-ni-verse, we eventually discover that it's we who have been our own best friend all along. All those twelve Light Beings are You and me, too. All the angels are You and me. All the demons. All the boxes. All the open spaces. All the differences are all part of the same thing.

In the motionless silence of blissful beingness, in the eternal field of light that is pure awareness, all is the same. All is pure potential. All is pure spirit. In the ripples of motion, from cosmic energy to wind to waves to the flesh of your own fingers, all is still the original light, manifesting its potential in the context of time and space to experience itself. You are the light, and you are the limits. You are the I in I am.

I am the box, and I am outside of the box, I am, I am. And so are You. And you.

22

Which Way?

I can think of my own individual existence as being metaphorically represented by a tree. My soul is the trunk, with its roots reaching into a vast source, and this lifetime is the route I have traveled from branch to smaller branch to twig, toward one of thousands of leaves. As a human defined by linear time, I am like an ant: each time I veer onto one branch, I have left another unexplored, and only one leaf will be my final destination. As a being living in more dimensions, I am like a bird: I can fly from branch to branch, touch any of the many leaves, my many lives' outcomes, that all exist at once.

I can look at humanity the same way. God, the God who listens and talks to us and seems to have a personality, is the trunk, sprouting upward from the universe, which is a Beingness beyond personality, a Source beyond definition. The trunk branches outward into archangels and ascended masters and the rest of the spiritual hierarchy, and then perhaps into group souls before individualizing into single souls, where each of us is a leaf within touching distance of other leaves.

With this concept of humanity in mind, I once traced my particular branch backwards, took a different turn, and found myself briefly exploring someone else's life.

The father of my stepchildren lost his older sister when she was nine. Bill could remember almost nothing about Mary, even though he was eight when she was killed by a truck while riding her bicycle. He believed he was harboring a deep sadness that was affecting his present feelings about relationships, but neither talking nor meditating had unlocked the reservoir of emotion.

I didn't know what to expect when I went in search of his memories for him one afternoon while he was working. Sitting quietly in my living room, with my eyes closed, I imagined myself going back along a branch on the tree of humanity, until I came to the snapped-off twig that was Mary's short life. Then I moved forward along her lifeline.

Images started coming to me. I was climbing a stairway inside a house, heading for a bedroom on the second floor. I heard someone, an adult woman, Mother, calling from downstairs that M was on her way over. In the hallway was a bicycle. It was blue, a small girl's bike with a white wicker basket between the handlebars.

I seemed to be viewing memories, in the same somewhat vague way I can recall some of my own, with a dreamlike quality around the edges. But these were not my memories. Mary would have been about my age if she had lived, so I assumed that there was no reincarnation involved. Was I really capable of tapping into someone else's memories?

When Bill came home, I asked him if he remembered anyone visiting his childhood house whose name started with an M.

"M?" he repeated. "M. Oh, Em! Yes! Emma! We called her Em. She was our babysitter! Oh, my, I haven't thought about her in so many years."

"Did Mary have a bedroom on the second floor?" Encouraged by his response, I told him what I had tried to do, and described what I had seen of the inside of the house.

"Yes!" He told me where his room was, too, the one he had shared with his brothers.

"Then I saw a blue bicycle," I told him.

"Mary's bike was blue," he said, his voice faltering, his eyes filling with tears. He looked at me. No, he was looking through me. "It had a white basket on the front." Suddenly he was sobbing, releasing a tremendous well of pain. He couldn't speak. The plug had been pulled. "I missed her so much." More memories and emotions poured forth, followed by wonderful insights.

I was pretty stunned by what had just happened.

A tree as the metaphor for one of the shapes of life's energy was re-enforced for me. But I hadn't yet applied this metaphor to the planet Earth, until I read a science fiction story about many Earths existing at the same time. It occurs to me that I've been an ant on the tree of Earth, choosing one path, toward one leaf, one version among many existing in a variety of dimensions or alternate realities.

Why? Why, of all the possibilities, from the darkest, grimmest version to the most blissful, have I chosen to focus on *this* version of Earth, the one that appears to be on the verge of crashing or soaring, of major self-destruction or major breakthrough into planetary awakening?

Okay, if I really could choose any version, and on some level I knew that I could, then I would have chosen this one because I love a challenge. I love participating in improvement. I wanted to outgrow judging reality as good or bad and this is the place to do it. I can come up with a lot of reasons.

But, wait a minute. As an ant on this tree of Earth, at every branching I have had only the choice of heading, ultimately, toward one particular leaf. My best version of Earth is still way ahead of me. If I were a bird, though, I wouldn't have to be limited by forward linear motion. I could choose any branch, any leaf, right away. So how masterful do I want to be? How much do I want to live in a greater set of dimensions? If I could choose any version of the world to live in right now, would I still choose the one that might possibly self-destruct?

No! I would choose one that is past the worst crisis, even if it hasn't noticed yet because things are still in turmoil. I would choose a version of the world that is, in spite of its faltering, truly unfolding its potential, actually giving birth to its entry into a greater set of dimensions, or better yet, becoming a responsible adolescent, or more, healing itself from disease and owning its gloriously masterful power to transform itself.

Do I have this choice?

I emailed a friend about this theory and told her that I'd decided to choose the version of the world that is already experiencing a major breakthrough into planetary consciousness.

I'd put my thought into words.

I shut down my computer, forgot what I'd been thinking about, and turned on the TV. I didn't have a TV guide, so I just waited to see what was on the channel that came on. The show in progress was a relatively new series I hadn't yet seen called *Mysterious Ways*. The plot unfolded: although the doctors could find no scientific cause for a piece of fabric which may have touched Jesus to be the agent for instant recoveries from fatal diseases, the main character believed in and demonstrated its effectiveness. People were miraculously healed.

Okay, so it was fiction, but I cheered. The public is evidently receptive to the idea being offered by these scriptwriters. The idea of miracles is being revived, outgrowing science's skeptical limits, igniting itself into the awareness of millions of viewers.

One of the commercials following the show plugged a product for cold sores. The product was advertised as activating a tingling sensation on the sore, but the slogan was, "Start to heal it as soon as you feel it." Wow, I thought, now there's an interesting way to phrase that message. It's not saying the *product* will heal the cold sore, it's saying *you* will. And it's saying something broader, too. It's an echo of at least a national, if not a worldwide, awareness that feeling your pain is the beginning of healing your pain. The slogan was repeated several times. "Start to heal it as soon as you feel it."

(Some part of me thinks that there are angels whispering into the ears of ad designers. They get the message through wherever they can. There are even angels of stupid ads. The ones that make you groan or grimace or laugh out loud at how bad they are? That's exactly the effect the angels were trying to achieve. The commercials are so pathetic no one would want to be caught dead buying the product.)

I took a kitchen break and noticed for the first time what was printed on my roll of paper towels. *Keep your promises. Seek out the good in people. Be forgiving of yourself and others.* On a roll of paper towels!

I decided to watch the next show that came on, as well. *Dateline* has won awards for its TV journalism, its reporting of events that are in fact happening on the planet. The theme was alternative healing methods. Two women with stage-four breast cancer, both assumed to be beyond rescue by any western-medicine means (in other words, expected to die) had agreed to try the herbal-remedy recommendations of a Tibetan healer.

One woman's outlook was positive and forward thinking. She wanted to see her daughter graduate from high school, she said with tears in her eyes. She wanted to see her daughter get married and have children. She followed the healer's advice to the letter. Her cancer stopped growing. At the end of a year on the program, she was convinced that she could beat the disease. She felt great.

The other woman, who, despite the Tibetan's instructions, continued to drink coffee and alcohol, often felt depressed and disheartened. Her disease slowly got worse. By the end of the year she wanted to revert to the western methods to try to prolong her life, even though the side effects would be painful.

Little attention was paid to the variables in each woman's life and attitude, and the outcomes were inconclusive, but the report ended with the suggestion that it would be a valuable undertaking to merge eastern and western methods of approaching disease and health.

I hadn't yet seen such coverage on a typical media show. I couldn't have felt more validated in my choice of an Earth version if I'd tuned in to the Dalai Lama on PBS.

If someone else had turned on the TV, though, looking for corroborating evidence of a collapsing civilization or dying planet, they would have found it. I can't deny that. So I don't quite know how to fit this Earth-as-tree metaphor into my present reality. It looks more like all the versions of Earth are in this one location, overlapping one another, and influencing one another.

Can I make this leap? Can I trust that if I choose to live on a planet that is bursting into new life, new hope, a new sense of responsibility and abundance, I will be doing so?

The next day, while driving, I happened to tune in to National Public Radio's *Car Talk*. The two brothers do a lot of joking as they answer calls about car problems, but one of them wasn't kidding when he said, "In the last year, five or six times, I have fixed cars by a laying on of hands."

His brother laughed, and then probably shrugged as he said, "Hey, you laughed at me when I said I did that."

"Yeah, but when you did it, it didn't work! When I did, it worked." He went on to describe one of the occasions. I started thinking about all the times I've just trusted my car to fix itself, and it has. And here someone was broadcasting this concept to millions of listeners!

The day after that, I was invited by a friend to attend a church I'd never heard of. Twelve ministers share sermon time over the course of a year. After this week's presentation about an unconditionally loving God who is supporting us in our awakening consciousness, more than a dozen healers rose and formed a tunnel with their uplifted arms in front of the pews. Every member of the congregation walked beneath the raised hands of the healers, receiving their blessings and loving energy.

Then the two ministers volunteered to do readings. One of them, a man in his sixties, looked around the room slowly. "Martha, you've recently had an inspiration, a new idea. Do you know what I'm talking about?" Martha did. "Good, because I don't, but I'm being told that you should go forward with it."

"Oh, good! Thank you!"

"You there, the man in black? You need to let go of your resentment. It will just eat away at you. Does this make any sense? Okay. I'm being told that you should just let all that go and move forward." He gave about ten readings, and then sat down.

The other minister, a redheaded woman, looked around the room. "The lady next to Jaqi." She was looking at me. I nodded. "You have a gentle spirit with you. A very loving spirit. I see an obstacle ahead, but then I see a kite flying. It's soaring." I smiled at the image. She went on to give readings to several other people as well.

I was blown away. This is a church?

After the meeting was over, a woman said to me, "Once those miracles start happening in your life, they just keep coming, don't they?"

During a recent train ride, three different people, unprompted by any suggestions from me, launched into long descriptions of near-death experiences, visitations from the other side, and messages from a higher power.

Am I bumping into the most confirming evidence I could possibly ask for, just because this is what I wanted?

I don't know. The way my life used to be would make me doubt it. Whenever I yearned for something because the lack of it made me ache, by the time I got it, it almost didn't matter if I had it or not, because I'd meanwhile found ways to accommodate the lack. It was wonderful to have it, but I was already happy without it. It almost seemed that it was because I was happy without it that it came to me. Eventually I realized that there is only one thing I can't live without. And that one thing isn't air or food or money or love or a peaceful planet. It's me. My soul. My essence. My knowing that I am complete, beyond my body. As long as I have that, and all it entails -- my sense of oneness with the infinite and eternal multiverse, my love of the mystery and miracle of existence -- as long as I know who I am, really, it doesn't matter whether I can choose a version of Earth or must abide by Earth's choices for herself. And maybe because it doesn't matter, Earth will choose to be loved, and to encourage love among all the members of her family. When I look outside the window at the hills graced with sleeping trees and fields of snow, when I hear the frogs sing, when I witness human longing and human courage, when I think of my children and the children all over the world, I hope so. I hope this exquisitely beautiful planet not only survives, but thrives. I hope the somewhere that we long to be is here.

It's so easy to get caught up in the cynicism and fear-mongering, even that of well-intentioned environmentalists, who cry against the deforestation of the planet, the extinction of hordes of species, the polluting of rivers. I can be soberingly convinced that our world is beyond hope of rescue. Or I can understand that mankind, too, is just another force of Nature. How many hundreds or thousands of times has the planet been devastated by asteroids or thrown into localized ice ages by global shifts? How many times have tropical paradises been swept into deserts by tidal waves, earthquakes, and volcanic upheavals that destroyed species and forests and landscapes? And how many hundreds or thousands of times have new species evolved, new forests spread across what was once an inland sea, fresh waters meandered across charred stretches of blackened bodies? Humanity itself has been indomitable for hundreds of thousands of years, despite the cataclysms. Even as the environmentalists are predicting doom, researchers and designers and scientists are coming up with more ways to harness natural renewable energy sources than ever before. According to an article in *Lapis* magazine, politicians and economists are discovering that promoting and investing in renewable resources are popular and profitable actions. Could there be better news? We don't even have to expect ourselves to lose our lust for power or our greed for profit! Both are already beginning to serve the best interests of everyone involved.

The somewhere I long for — is it here?

It depends on which part of me is doing the longing. If a forest burns down or a city collapses in an earthquake, this little me can't push this version of Earth into another reality where that forest still grows or that city remains intact. But I can live in a greater reality, where everything that once existed still exists, if that's what I need in order to feel whole, or where everything keeps on changing, if I'm okay with that. My personal fear or despair is not a responsible contribution to the planet. If I am driven to do something about the problems I see, then my actions help to create the world that I want to live in, but if my natural inclination is to tell a story or to bake a cake, then my contribution is the responsibility I take for being one less iota of indifference and one more of appreciation.

I can choose to align myself with what feels good, day by day, moment by moment, and remember that what feels good includes both surrender and intention. As the redheaded minister said when she concluded her talk, "May I be granted the serenity to accept what I cannot change, the courage to change what I can, and the wisdom to know that the *what* is me!"

Living on a planet that rotates from night into day and revolves from winter into spring doesn't have to be an experience of opposites or dichotomies. Nor does it have to follow a linear time. Not if I embrace all of who I really am.

When we live it and love it and create it from inside all these different skins, it's full of dunkin' donuts and deer hunters and devils, angels and apple cider and astronauts.

But when the veil is lifted and the vision is complete, then all of the information in-forming this vast quantum-foam mind-at-large into all these differentiated sounds and colors and beings -- all of this infinite and eternal Intelligence -- is already experiencing itself in all possible ways, forever. S/H/We are already, always have been, always will be somewhere. We don't have to wait to get there. We don't have to long to be somewhere. We are already here.

23

Refreshments Are Available

Youngsters, newly arrived souls, and older ones who are in need of a refresher course because you seem to have misplaced your original instructions, I will be substituting for your instructor today. Your regularly scheduled instructor will return shortly.

If you find my assumptions about what you might have forgotten upon arrival inapplicable, please feel free to leave.

As per the original instructions, I can assure you again:

There is nothing that you will have to learn that you will not have to unlearn.

You will not be tested. You will only be shown what you are made of. Refreshments are available.

Those of you who have decided to remain, please have a seat, put away your notebooks, and pull out your mirrors, for, as many of us have discovered, this place appears to be a house of mirrors. Whether the world out there is a reflection of what's going on in these bodies, or these internal experiences are a reflection of the outer world, we seem to be up against a mirror, and it takes some getting used to, moving around on whichever side of the mirror we happen to find ourselves in.

Alice, our astute friend from Wonderland, discovered on one side of the looking glass that to get to the house on the hill she saw ahead of her, she had to walk backwards. This same technique of reversal might prove itself to be just the trick, when you find yourselves in a tricky situation.

Permit me to offer you an example.

To make less of a fear, make more of it.

I'd been in this body for fifteen years when I accidentally stumbled upon this particular aspect of this handy technique.

I was accompanying my five-year-old sister on her first Ferris wheel ride. I wasn't crazy about the Ferris wheel myself, but she was eager to climb aboard. We latched ourselves in, me with trepidation, and little Celia with excitement. We were lifted into the air. Our seat lurched up and over empty space, dangling precariously, and then dropped. At the unexpected sensation of finding her stomach in her throat, Celia stiffened with fear. I pretended I was having fun, hoping that my pretense would be contagious, but as we came up and around the second time, she scrunched her eyes shut, braced herself, held her breath, and held on till her knuckles whitened, enduring the drop until she could speak. "Make them stop, Lesta! Please make them stop! I want to get off!"

The Ferris wheel was on a roll, and, being on the shy side, I wasn't convinced that I could flag the man at the helm in time to prevent another lurch over empty space. "It's really scary when we go over the top, isn't it?" Her admission had helped me voice my own discomfort. More for her sake than mine, since I was already into enduring by then, I came up with an idea. "Let's try something. Let's pretend that when we get to the top, we want to go even further. We want to fly, like Superman. We want to see everything we can see, the whole amusement park, from even higher up."

"Okay," Celia said in a tiny voice.

We approached the top, and both of us leaned forward. "Come on, let's go higher! Higher!" we shouted together. We wanted to fly!

The drop down, this time, was a mere disappointment, a postponement of our next opportunity to stretch ourselves and look around at all the lights and the people and the other rides. Somehow we'd slipped through the looking glass to the other side. We still didn't want our seat to drop, but if that's what it took to get around to the peak of the cycle again, well then, okay. We had taken what we feared further than it could take us, and we found ourselves beyond it, looking back at it, and laughing. "That was fun! Let's do it again!"

You can probably think of other ways in which this technique might work when you can't figure out which side of the mirror you're stuck in.

To feel more connected, share your sense of isolation.

To reclaim yourself, give yourself away. Reveal who you are, and in the revealing, discover yourself.

To become invincible, be vulnerable. Bare your needs. Discover that your needs met fill you up and make you stronger, and that your needs unmet empty you out and make you stronger.

To overcome a loss, undergo the loss. Feel how much you don't want this loss. Feel how much you will die from this loss. Feel yourself dying. Feel yourself losing your mind, your sense of security, your will. Take the loss even further than it can take you. And you will discover that you have fallen into a black hole and have come out on the other side into more than you could have imagined.

To get out of what you're in, go into it.

To expand into infinite consciousness, focus on the infinitely small within you.

And the next time you're stuck and can't figure out which reversal will help you pierce the looking glass, take a look in that mirror you're holding up and tell yourself that you are only a reflection of what you're looking at. If that turns you inside out, reverses which is world and which is you, well, then, you do remember after all. You've done exactly what you came here to do. You've dissolved the looking glass.

Okay, another helpful hint, for those of you who might have forgotten your inner voicemail password when you arrived. You know you came equipped with an inner voice to keep you connected to where we've all come from, and you know it's accessible, but how do you tap into it, and how do you distinguish it from all the static interference?

The reason it's so easy to overlook, in case you've forgotten, is that it feels as natural to you as your own normal body temperature or the taste of your own tongue. Nothing is amiss, there's nothing drawing your attention to it, the aaahhhh of comfort is as unheeded as the sound of air being breathed in and out. The easiest way to discern it, unfortunately, is to notice when it's being drowned out, when, instead of vaguely hearing mmm, you're clearly hearing "Shouldn't have," or "Uh, oh," or "Ouch!"

If you listen to the way your health, or your favorite music, or someone's comforting companionship simply belongs to you in the most deeply satisfying way, you'll be listening to the language of your inner voice. It speaks in terms of Okay.

When you're uncertain, scan the mixed messages. The ones that come through as "Must do," "Have to have," or "Don't even dare" are not your inner voice. Just keep scanning until what you hear is so familiar to your total sense of well-being that it doesn't have to advertise itself at all, it just offers you an Okay. Okay, you need to yell and scream right now. Okay, you need to make that move. Okay, it's time to sleep on it. Okay, what you are feeling is your truth. Okay, the password is that simple. Okay, you can relax now. Okay.

If you're having difficulty with your system, let me remind you that there is a back-up: the outer voice. Life is still carrying on a conversation with you, even though you might have stopped noticing it, having been overwhelmed by the sensory overload in parts of the planet. If you converse with Life, yell and plead and sing and insist and express your hopes and tell it your intentions, you'll hear it, responding as it always has. Whatever you expect, desire, fear, resist, or feel grateful for, the answer is the same: *Okay*. I don't like this job! *Okay*. I'm afraid I'll never get ahead. *Okay*. Give me some options here! *Okay*. I need some help with this. *Okay*. I think I'd like a different job. *Okay*. I'm ready for it now! *Okay!*

Okay?

This next reminder is for those of you who are witnessing confusion in your surroundings because you haven't noticed that you've already activated the best piece of equipment you brought with you, your power of transformation.

I beg your pardon? Yes, you activated your power of transformation as soon as you arrived. Yesterday you transformed pita and pasta, or pizza and Pepsi, into blood and bones and body heat. You probably didn't notice, because it was so easy you didn't even have to think about it. That's generally how the power of transformation works, although it works just as effectively when you do think about it.

I've discovered that although I usually like to adhere to a healthy diet, when I get a craving for junk food, if I think about it and ask my body to use what it can on a molecular level and not to retain anything from the emotional and chemical levels, it seems happy to comply. Your body is capable of transforming whatever you are capable of expecting it to transform.

You've been using your emotions as tools of transformation all along. Last week your anger, which you wielded like a torch, created a distance between yourself and someone who was hurting you, because that was exactly what you needed to do at the moment. You have also wielded that torch to clear away old debris, unclutter an area for new growth.

You have made good use of depression. The name implies its use. It's a shovel. You made a dent in that layer, beneath which was buried something that needed air, and when you kept digging deeper, you opened up a whole new space inside yourself and found it easier to breathe again.

You've changed your whole day with a good laugh.

Whenever you're stumped about which emotional tool of transformation to use, you can, with your intentions, resort to that all-purpose one, of course: love. I love being an idiot! I love being a nobody! I love being rejected! I love being lonely! I wanna be lonely again, doo be doo be dooo...

You've been transforming the people around you. Scientists didn't know until they peered all the way down into quantum particles that nothing can be observed without being changed by the observer. In the meantime, your observations have been changing everyone around you, all along. When you noticed something beautiful about the checkout girl the other day, you made her feel more beautiful, even if you didn't voice your observation. When you realized that behind your co-worker's need to compete was the need for a personal victory to lift his self-esteem, you helped him realize a truer version of himself. When you noticed that your friend didn't mean to hurt you, but to protect herself, you transformed her stance in the world.

I was transformed by the snowplow man one winter day in PA.

He had plowed my driveway all the way up to my studio, but the snow on that last bit of slope hid a large patch of ice. His truck started to lose traction, went sliding backwards over the embankment, and ended up in a shallow hollow among the brambles and trees. Since it was sunk into the snow at quite an angle, I offered to call my neighbor to bring his tractor and winch to the rescue, but this man, who had his ten-year-old son with him, said he was a "never-say-die kinda guy." He wanted to try to get the truck back up onto the driveway on its own power. I didn't think he had a chance, but my step-daughter Raine, finding his positive attitude contagious, wanted to help him try, so we all dug away the snow and shoveled gravel under the tires. Every time he would rock the truck and just about get the front tires up to the rim of the embankment, the tires would spin on the icy leaves and mud. Raine's sister-in-law Lisa joined us, and we all shoveled more gravel and cheered him on, but the truck just kept losing it and sliding even further back into the brambles. I offered again to get help, thinking there was no way this was going to work, but this guy had an undaunted determination to climb out of this hole. He kept telling us to stay positive. So Lisa and Raine and I started yelling to the truck, "Come on, baby, come on, you can do it!"

Thirty-five minutes into our effort, with no let-up of cheerful confidence on the driver's part, I wanted so badly to prove him right, especially for his son's sake, that it finally occurred to me we'd been going about it the wrong way. As the truck rocked back and forth, once again spinning its wheels, I shouted to Raine and Lisa, "I know what we have to do! We have to *envision* the truck up there in the driveway! We have to look at that spot and *see* the truck there." With calm ferocity the three of us *intended* that truck to be where we were pointing. Two seconds later the truck went vroom and pulled right up over the incline and into the space we were looking at! *Okay!*

The snowplow man was blown away. He thanked us profusely for our help, but it was he who had transformed a potentially frustrating experience into a triumphant victory, and three possible doubters into surprised masters of visualization.

You are constantly transforming everyone you interact with.

You have also been transforming what the previous generation gave you. Compare yourself to your own parent at the same age, and you will see how much the values have changed. If you like what you see, you have already been contributing to what humanity needs next. It needs you to value yourself. If you don't, it is never too late to use your power of transformation with specific intention.

You have been transforming the planet. Every tree that uses its natural gift of producing oxygen adds to the atmosphere in which all of life survives. Every one of us who is breathing out, and as I look around I can see that all of you are doing so, is adding to the atmosphere needed by the trees. Every one of us who is being fully alive is adding to the atmosphere in which the soul thrives.

Waldorf teachers are encouraged to think about, as they're falling asleep, the children who missed school that day, and it is not an uncommon experience for them to be told, the following day, both by the absentees and by their classmates, that the absent children already received that part of the lesson. They relate the details of the missed chapter with the absolute conviction that the teacher went over it with them personally.

You are transforming everything you touch, listen to, look at, and think about. Your power of transformation is never *not* active!

With your permission, I'll offer you one more reminder.

It is not your brain that determines what your body does. Your brain is simply the relay between your soul-mind and your body. Your soul-mind is what connects you to where we come from. Since condensing yourself into this narrow set of dimensions temporarily squeezed a lot out of you – you're not just a recovering soldier or a recovering corporate cog, you're a recovering newborn – you would probably find it enhancing to expose yourself frequently to suggestions of what is possible.

A group of addicts was told by a therapist that every chemical they were using to try to recapture pleasure was already being produced by their brains. The therapist didn't know if this was entirely true, but she had enough evidence that it was at least in part true; she was winning their confidence by giving them the credit they deserved for seeking pleasure; and she was convinced enough of her positive motive to be convincing. She asked them to instruct their brains to accumulate the necessary amount of their preferred chemical, and then, on cue, to release it into their bodies. Every single one of them instantly got high. She was able to transfer their dependence on drugs to the actual pleasure-producing power of their soul-minds.

The instant success, I think, was due to the familiarity of feeling high. Their brains knew how to translate the instructions into the desired effect because the desired effect had recently been experienced. It has been more difficult for people to produce the ultimate high of enlightenment for themselves because it has been merely described by those who claim to have attained it, and it has been described as taking years to achieve. It hasn't been experienced as a memory of our own. In truth, the high of enlightenment is totally easy to experience, and once experienced, easy to induce again and again, and once desired, easy to maintain, in and around and behind our mundane activities and human emotions. It is our natural state. It is what we are recovering into.

Recovering implies gaining again. We are not becoming, we're remembering what we've always been, the dark and the light. We are the particles and the waves, and we are the invisible field from which they spring. We are the interface of matter and perception, and we are the limitless ethereal source of potential. We are the nuances and explosions of change, and we are the bliss of absolute tranquility. We are the infinite cosmic intelligence discovering and creating itself, and we are the eternally still and silent present beyond all space and time.

We are what is beyond impossible, making itself possible.

The suggestions of what is possible are all around you. But then, you have already been availing yourselves of them. That's why you're here! And the planet is cheering!

If you have any questions, or need any further elucidation concerning your stay on the planet, your regularly scheduled instructor is now available for conference. Just look into that dissolving mirror -- or log in to your inner voicemail. Okay?

And, *please,* help yourself to refreshments.

24

Pushed and Pulled

When my daughter, who had traveled through various countries looking for a place that felt like home, called me and told me she had finally found it, I listened to her story with growing excitement. Because a friend of mine had recently asked me to edit her autobiography, which included her six-month transformation on Maui, I was already eager to hear how Fawni had responded to the energy of the island. It had welcomed her with its open-armed aloha spirit by producing what seemed to be magical encounters. She was actually told by one person that she was in alignment with Maui's energy and should be living there.

If she was going to move to Maui, could I visit her during the winter months? "Yes, Ma!" A week later I had to revise my options. How would she feel about me moving to Maui with her? Her enthusiasm was more than gratifying, it was the invitation to listen to an unmistakable message.

The day after her phone call in early February, eastern PA was hit by the third ice storm of the season. The three-story "treehouse" that had once been my art studio, had later served as a party retreat for my growing teenagers, was then transformed into a living space for each of my three maturing step-children, and was now being rented by a dear friend of mine, was situated among tall hickories, oaks, and maples. A branch had broken off under the weight of the ice and crashed through an arched plexiglass window on the second floor. Since the driveway had become a solid sheet of ice, making it impossible for a repairman to tackle the tricky job of fixing the two-foot-wide hole, my friend and I did our best to cover it with a tarp. My first thought was one of dismay. There's no way I can leave for the winter. I'm responsible for this property. What if the pipes freeze again, what if there's some other predictable or unexpected damage, who would make sure there's enough firewood for the only sources of heat in both the studio and my earth-sheltered house? My second thought was a break-through. What if this is an indication that something needs to change? What if after thirty years of enduring the damp cold and the long dark hours of winter, I decided to sell my house and move to a warmer climate? What if I'm actually being pushed off my property for some reason even beyond my own need for comfort?

As soon as my daughter and I agreed that moving to Maui was the plan, I was inundated with confirmation that this was the right decision. An acquaintance stopped by and described the life-changing retreat she had just attended in Hawaii. I found an unopened box in my hall closet that had accompanied the water softener I'd had installed a few years before to prevent further corrosion of the plumbing; I opened it up, curious about what I had overlooked for so long — it contained bars of ecologically friendly soap in a package labeled *Island Paradise*. I drove through a nearby town on an unseasonably warm day and passed a man on the sidewalk whose T-shirt had printed across its back the large word MAUI.

Although my house would not sell for another two years, which meant that I would be living on a less-than-meager social security income and my credit card, our arrival in Maui, about nine months after the seed of change had been planted, was initiated with the kind of magic I would gradually begin to assume was a possible way of life. The plumeria-scented tropical breeze that greeted us as we walked along the open-air corridor of the airport was life-enhancing. The car we'd leased from a local Rent-a-Heap outfit was waiting in the parking lot, unlocked — the paperwork, we were told, could wait till morning. The night attendant at the hostel asked if we'd ever been to Maui before. Yes, when Fawni was twelve, she and my mother and I had spent a week here, and yes, Fawni had visited this year. "Welcome back!" he said. "Maui missed you!" The next morning, as we filled out the rental car papers, the guy said to us, "You do know there are parallel universes, right?"

I was definitely in the right place!

By magic, we were guided to find a home. By magic, we were led to a heiau (a stone-encircled sacred area) where a kahuna was leading a ceremony. She reminded us that no matter how many past lives had been an endurance of repression, this lifetime was about shining our light. We sent loving energy to the entire planet. As we left, I made a friend, Trudy, who introduced me to several other extraordinary women, with whom we eventually formed a circle that began to meet every two weeks to share our spiritual awareness.

Trudy alerted me to a shamanic workshop — something not readily available in my former Pennsylvania Dutch community — during which we met up with our power animals. I had already become spontaneously aware of a silver she-wolf many years before — she had seemed to roll out of me one morning as I emerged from a dream state, and led me to where I saw my sister crying, which, as it turned out, was exactly what was happening at exactly that moment — so my envisioned encounter with this spirit animal was a happy reunion. To remind myself that alternate realities are available to us, during the next week I painted the blue-eyed wolf and hung the painting on my bedroom wall.

I took a class called Crystal Manifestation, during which we were guided by the teacher to call in assistance from ethereal beings to energize our intentions. Being so filled to the brim with gratitude for everything Maui was offering me, I could never think of what to ask for, so I usually asked that everyone else's desires be fulfilled. But observing the seriousness with which Ev called in our higher selves and other beings from higher realms, I began to reconsider the twelve Beings of Light that had given me such valuable gifts so many years ago. Were they just extensions of my own vivid imagination, abstractions of information rising from my own subconscious or descending from my own super-conscious self? Or did they actually exist somewhere in this universe? I decided to ask that very question in my journal, and then I heard the dictation that often comes in so rapidly that I don't know what I've written until I read it again.

"Remember the signs that you have been given all along. We are your multidimensional fractal self. We experience the density of flower, sea, and tree through you, as you experience the rare-air holographic Creative Dream through us. As you believe in the presence of your own body, believe in us. As you believe in the existence of an infinite and eternal mystery, believe in us. As you believe in a silver she-wolf guiding you to your sister in need, believe in

us. As You believe in Your Power to Create Infinitely, grant us the reality of being that is granted to every bit of creation, from cockleshell to cauliflower, from cuttlefish to Eiffel tower. We do exist. Each of us fluctuates in form, in content, in identity, as multidimensional godlings of unlimited freedom. You are an aspect of us. We cannot nor would we ever consider to abandon you any more than you would abandon your hand, which helps you to perceive and to create. We shift to communicate with you through whoever or whatever is available. Accept the reality of what You create. The point in accepting the unreality of your world is to equalize it to the reality of our world. It is all pure Consciousness. It is all real. We are here. WE ARE HERE."

The next day, as I was driving back to my house from the beach, along the residential street I had been taking walks on for over a year by then, I suddenly had to brake, because out from a side street was trotting a wolf. What?? A wolf on Maui?! The collarless silver creature paused in front of my stopped car. I rolled down my window and spoke to her. "What are you doing here?" She came over to me, and I reached out and petted her, mesmerized by her beautiful blue eyes.

And so the demarcations between realities dissolved. I had just been reminded of my spirit animal, and there she was, not a possibly imagined creature in a trance-induced realm, but a tangible living presence in this supposedly solid world. I had never seen this animal in this area before, and I would not see her again, but her appearance had been so uncannily timely that I went back and read my journal entry again, this time noticing that the use of the words you and You altered in meaning who or Who was being addressed. I also noticed the mention of the wolf, and slowly the message sank in. It is all real. We are all co-creators of our realities.

And once we understand that, the gap of time between thought and manifestation begins to close. A few months later, my cousins were visiting the island, and as they were leaving my house to go exploring, they told me that just that morning they had seen a pueo, an owl who is considered, in Hawaiian lore, to be a guardian or protector. "Oh, I've never seen one. I hope I do get to see one soon. Have fun exploring! See you later." I closed the door behind them, and opened it again when I heard them shouting my name. "Lesta! There's an owl in your driveway!"

That I had been pushed to leave Pennsylvania and pulled to come to Maui was becoming a magnetic affair of the heart. I am in love with this mysterious and magical island!

25

Painted Messages

What I had to offer Maui in return for all the gifts I had been receiving gradually became apparent.

I knew already, as I've mentioned in an earlier chapter, that it was possible as an artist to open up to messages for others, to translate into visible images colorful confirmations of their ineffable experiences.

In fact, a few years before leaving PA, I'd had the opportunity not only to be open to whatever might come through for someone else, but to ask specifically for applicable information.

My friend Fran met her husband Guy in high school. They had been married for over forty years when Guy, who was also her best friend, was killed while riding his motorcycle, in a head-on collision with an SUV driven by a teenaged girl. He died instantly.

Knowing that in her state of incredulous shock and unfathomable loss she would be inundated with grieving and concerned family and friends, I decided to wait a few days before contacting her. Doing so was on my mind every day, but I was not consciously thinking of her when I woke up at 2:30 am, four days later, feeling driven to start a painting.

The images that emerged on the canvas during the next three hours were of a man and woman, separated by half an arm's-length but connected heart to heart, flying together over a tiny blue orb. Beneath them (they appeared to be viewed from above) was the entrance to a light-filled tunnel. Ahead of them the tunnel opened into a widening empty space. Flowing back from the head of the man was a swirl of energy that struck me as resembling the head of a zebra, and I found myself turning the canvas over and writing on the back, "Even zebras get the blues."

I left the canvas on the easel and went back to sleep for a few hours, and when I returned later in the morning, I saw the painting from across the room and gasped. Formed within the outlines of the two people was Fran's distinctively heart-shaped face, her eyes downcast, her mouth contracted in sorrow.

"Oh my gosh," I whispered, feeling something prickle through me. "Guy, if you're here," I said out loud, for the first time finding myself consciously and specifically requesting that I be used for a channel through my art, "come through. If you have messages for Fran…" Instantly I squeezed some white acrylic paint onto the palette, dabbed a narrow brush into it, and didn't know if my eyes were open or closed as the brush pulled my hand to the empty space above the flying couple and squiggled around for a few seconds. After I dropped the brush into the jar of water, I looked at the canvas, staring through sudden tears at Guy's face in miniature, the familiar tiny smile beneath his mustache, the upturned eyebrows, and an all-too-typical wave of his hand from beside his cheek. "Okay," I breathed, barely grasping the full impact of what was happening, "if there's anything you want to communicate in words, Guy, please make use of me, right now. I'm open."

I grabbed the marker and wrote down what I heard him say on the back of the canvas. "Tell her I love her. Tell them all. God, you know?" "I'm not that far away." "Fly with me."

It wasn't until days later that Fran was ready to have me and a mutual friend visit. She fell into my arms and cried softly. Then she pulled back and asked, "What's this?" about the painting I'd brought into her house. "Fran, I think Guy is still around," I said.

"I think so, too," she said. "I saw him in the doorway that night. He was crying. But maybe it was just a dream. Or maybe I'm going crazy. I feel crazy. But he was crying because he didn't want to leave."

"He hasn't left," I told her. I explained what had happened as I showed her her own face on the canvas, and his.

"It's Guy!" She held the canvas with both hands and kissed his face. I told her about the messages on the back, and as she read them, she suddenly held her heart and staggered to a chair, tears flowing. " 'Fly with me?!' On our wedding day we gave one another a plaque – it was a silly joke of a gift, some airline motto – that said 'Come fly with me.' On our wedding day!"

It wasn't only Fran who let herself begin to believe that Guy was still around. Her three grown daughters no longer wondered if it was okay for their mother to find comfort in talking with their father. Other messages came through from other friends. They came through in songs that almost seemed to have been written by him for Fran. Punctuating the undulations of grief, anger, and agony that naturally arose from what still felt like an amputation, a growing acceptance of continuity began to prevail. But neither Fran nor her daughters could make any sense, Fran told me later, of that one phrase on the back of the painting, "Even zebras get the blues." Her daughters had even Googled it in hopes of finding some clue to its relevance, and I, meanwhile, somewhat overcome by the privilege of having been made use of as so clear a channel, had neglected to make a distinction between that first phrase and the messages I'd specifically requested from Guy.

"Lesta, did you hear what happened?" a mutual friend asked me over the phone seven months later. "Fran wants to tell you herself, I know, but I just have to share this much with you. Her daughter was at an art show, and she saw this painting of a zebra, and she read the name of the artist, and, are you ready for this? It was done by the girl who was driving the vehicle that killed Guy."

I was flooded with an inexpressible wave of comprehension and gratitude. It wasn't just the phrase that made sense. It was the whole Universe. I shared awe-inspired tears with Fran over the phone as she confided, "We've all been on this weird high. This is so mind-boggling." She related the details of her daughter's staggering discovery and their subsequent decision. Katie was a student counselor at the same high school where the seventeen-year-old driver of the SUV (she had been driving for only two weeks) was a senior. Katie had been purposely avoiding the girl, still acutely feeling her own grief and anger, but was in the hall speaking with another counselor when the senior stopped to speak briefly with the other woman. "I'm sorry about that," the other counselor said afterwards, fully aware of the reason for Katie's conflicted emotions, but adding, "She's having a really rough time of it. She's been cutting herself." Katie couldn't manage getting involved, she had enough to deal with. She turned and found herself walking past a student art exhibition. Apparently the assignment had been to depict animals. Noticing a zebra on a blue background, she glanced at the name of the artist, which at that moment only fueled her need to distance herself. It wasn't until she was halfway down the hall that she mentally slapped her own forehead. "Oh my God! It's a ZEBRA!"

Fran and Katie decided to do something that they couldn't even imagine considering before. They hoped to meet with seventeen-year-old Brooke. They wanted to tell her they didn't blame her. They wanted the healing process to extend itself to someone whom they felt should not be blaming herself. And, if she was open to it, they wanted to tell her why.

Although I'd had a number of paintings turn out to be meaningful messages, I was not intending to carry on with that practice now that I was in Hawaii. It happened without my even anticipating it.

Following my first opportunity to display my work on Maui, which was at a group show at the Unity Church, I was approached by a German woman who asked me if I would be willing to do a portrait of her. She had never had one done before, but she was drawn to the spiritual nature of my work and thought that I would be able to capture a truer likeness of her than even photographs had been able to do.

Presented with this daunting challenge, I invited L to my cottage and told her that it would be easier for me to work from photographs, so rather than have her pose for several days to be painted directly, we spent an hour or so talking while I occasionally took a photo with my digital camera. I could see a sadness in her, and she admitted to me that ever since she had been a child, she had had a recurring longing to die. I also sensed a repressed desire to believe in an expanded version of reality, which she unwittingly confirmed by relating an occasion in which she met with derision when she mentioned an extrasensory awareness of an entity present in the room, causing her to actively ignore any further such shaming flights of fancy.

Looking through the photos after she left, I chose two that spoke to me of the divided nature of her self-acceptance. In the foreground was her present sixty-something self, which, as I painted the image, even though it resembled her quite accurately, began to look as if another version of herself was trying to come through. Behind that figure was a depiction of her most childlike expression, looking upwards toward a source of light.

When she returned to my cottage to pick up the portrait, I watched her walk up my short driveway with the same slow heaviness in her step I had noticed before. She came in and sat down on the couch, and I showed her the portrait. Happy to see her eyes light up at the sight of it, I explained to her what I had sensed as I worked on it.

"I had the strong impression, L, that you've had a past life as a Native American. If you imagine a cloth headband across the forehead, you could be looking at a Navajo woman."

"Oh! Oh, that is really strange, for you to say that. I had a past life regression once, and the clearest one that came through was exactly what you are telling me — it was a life as an Indian, in one of the Pueblo tribes of the Southwestern United States."

"Okay, wow." I hadn't known that. "Look at that wise elder of her tribe. She has been through so much, she has seen so much, and yet she has such a gentle presence. She is a beautiful woman." Not wanting to embarrass her by calling too much attention to the beauty I could see in her, I went on. "The other thing that came through really strongly, L, is that the child self within you is the one who wants to go back to where we all come from. She longs to return to that Love and Light, and that feels like a desire to die, which can be depressing. But you have a good many years, if you want to, to explore this life, so maybe it's time to have a conversation with that child self. Tell her how much you love her, how safe she is under your protection, and how much you would enjoy her helping you to become playful and full of wonder."

I went on to tell her about my own experiences of sensing entities around or meeting with those on the other side through dreams. Because she told me that this portrait was indeed a better likeness of her than any she had seen before, I felt emboldened to play the role of welcoming gatekeeper, inviting her into the realm of mystery, and she began to share some of what she had kept to herself for a lifetime to avoid others' opinions of her sanity. Before she left, she promised me — but really, the promise was to herself — that she was going to have a conversation with her little girl self. We hugged, and as I watched her go down the driveway to her car, carrying her portrait, my eyes widened at the unexpected sight. She was bouncing, almost dancing, like a happy child.

Another painting proved to be a communication between a friend and her deceased mother. I had sent several images by email to my group of women friends on Maui, accompanying each image with a poem. Next to the one of a woman standing with her back to the viewer, her arms raised, waving batons as butterflies danced and angelic spirits hovered around and above her, I had written

I thought of her as a conductor,
harmonizing with the elementals
eliciting the music of the butterflies
interacting with a choir of angels
until one day I saw her differently
she was unfolding
and enfolding
all of her own other aspects
her past and future lives
her many selves
into an inner chorus of integrity

Kati emailed me back that she was sure this was a message from her mother, who had often called Kati her little Butterfly, and who had mentioned to Kati that in her next life — in a future incarnation — she wanted to be a conductor!

I left the painting on Kati's porch. Sometimes no conversation is needed at all, just the satisfaction of being a "stealth donor."

I love being this instrument!

All of what we perceive through our five ordinary senses are interpretations of interference patterns rippling between the wavelengths of what we receive and what we emit. The freedom to use our imagination as one of our senses, as one of the points of reference where input and interpretation become perception, broadens our experience. We can enter a realm of cosmic music and prophetic visions and sensitivity to inter-dimensional beings and conversations with nature divas, a realm that was long denied to a generation reprimanded for daydreaming in a public institution geared toward creating a work force. This is what I'm discovering is the purpose behind any of us who are intuitive, creative, inspired to do healing work or energy work: we are sensing the shift, building the bridges, opening the floodgates, so that lives can be lived in the wild divine freedom of limitless potential.

26

Dreamtime Travelers

There are any number of videos on Youtube conveying the authenticity of remote viewing. Remote viewers, their training once promoted by the military, have branched out into private experiments that reveal the history of the Great Pyramid, the cataclysm that changed Mars from a populated planet to a desert, the complicated events that led to the 9/11 disaster, the ancient presence of extraterrestrial beings on one of Saturn's moons. While I am not qualified to understand the method resulting in scientifically provable information that verifies even those perceptions that can't be traditionally checked out as tangibly real, I do have some sense of what can make such explorations possible. The comprehension began to bloom within me as I listened to a description of the differences between Space-Time and Time-Space.

Space-Time is what we generally perceive as the reality in which we are participating. It consists of three dimensions of Space and one dimension of Time. The three dimensions of Space all exist simultaneously, and although these dimensions of Space are constantly in flux, they are also a reliable constant, one we call geography or solid matter or the street we take to the grocery store. We use one dimension of Time, the present, to explore this continuous and omnipresent spacial expanse. It takes time to go from the living room to the bathroom. The living room remains as it is, the bathroom remains as it is, but our perception of what exists in our immediate and present environment changes with the movement we make from one place to another. (Time is simply movement; whether it's the movement of atoms or planets or humans aging from childhood into adults, time is the experience of motion and change. Time is actually the first of the four dimensions in which we normally exist. Without the dance of the sub-atomic particles, without the surge of the frequencies of electro-magnetic waves, without the temporal duration of the constituents of space, they would not exist — but that's another subject.) So we make use of one dimension of Time, the present, to travel around the three dimensions of Space, to interact with different parts of the ever-present width, breadth, and height of the planet, exploring miles of plateau or mountain peaks or subterranean caves.

Time-Space is just the opposite. It consists of three dimensions of Time and one dimension of Space. Time is the constant — the past, present, and future are all simultaneously existent, all part of an infinite time-scape of Now. One dimension of Space, no longer the cube or the line but a singular point of perception, is used to explore the realm of Time. That point of perception can travel freely through the present, which is as vast as the universe, or into the past, which also exists every-when, and even into the future of probable and possible outcomes all existing in the potential and ready to become the actual by being chosen to manifest in Space-Time.

The ability to remote-view might simply be the ability (acquired by those aforementioned experimenters through rigorous training) to flip from Space-Time to Time-Space.

It seems to me that what is being called the Fifth Dimension by those aspiring to ascend into another level of awareness might also be considered an inclusion of these two ways of experiencing reality. While being grounded in the "real world" of physical needs and social improvements and technical advances, we are also evolving into intuitively acute perceivers of inter-dimensional beings, we are developing empathic awareness of other species, having flashes of insight into remembered events and future possibilities, empowering ourselves to communicate telepathically with one another and with those whom we once thought of as past or passed over, understanding near-death experiences as glimpses into realms that exist in different sets of frequencies. If each hemisphere of the brain is equipped to interpret one of two kinds of reality, perhaps what we are doing is not so much evolving as simply availing ourselves of what we are already equipped with. Perhaps the shift that is so needed and is already in evidence is the rebalancing of this and that, male and female, visible and invisible, light and dark, human and divine, yin and yang, infinite Space within a single point and eternal Time within the present moment.

*　*　*

Ah, just when I think I've grasped a concept, along comes another experience that stretches my thinking, bends it around a corner, and leads me off into yet another direction.

Shortly after I had written my thoughts about remote viewing, I met with a friend who told me what had happened between her two sons. The younger brother had been surfing on the west shore of Maui, and a particularly powerful wave knocked him off his board and towed him under, rolling him downwards with such force that he assumed he was about to die. Eyes open to the distance between himself and the surface, he accepted with a sense of peace that ultimate probability, when a hand reached down and grabbed him and pulled him up to air and safety. To whom that hand might have been attached he could not fathom, until two weeks later, when his older brother, on the mainland, cautioned him to please be careful when he went surfing. He'd had a dream, the older brother told his sibling. "You were surfing, and you went under — you were in trouble — I had to reach down through the water and pull you out."

I shouldn't have been surprised to the point of feeling my eyes shimmer with tears. Maybe it wasn't surprise. Maybe when we are given confirmation that Love can reach through Dreamtime, no training required, and shift this reality, the tears are of wonder and gratitude.

Less than a week after hearing that we can do more than view, we can influence what happens across both time and space, I received an email from a man in Australia. He had found my website and was contacting me because he'd had a dream in which an "older lady" had said to him, "We are the Infinite and the Eternal, experiencing Itself." Remembering the words when he woke up, he Googled them, found my name, and was led to my website. The first entry that came up, when I later Googled the words myself, was that sentence in its entirety, quoted from the novel *No Victor in Disguise* by Lesta Bertoia. He wrote to tell me that the message had been personally meaningful to him, and he was going to buy my book.

Since I didn't remember having a dream about visiting someone in Australia, I have to leave my interpretation open. It could have been my timeless Dreamtime self, unbeknownst to me, aware of some distant person's readiness to expand himself into his own true nature. It could be that the Conscious Universe, or a more local step-down version of it, triggered what could be a two-way benefit: I had only recently begun to update and to consider publishing this book, and here was confirmation that my words might be meaningful to others. It could be that within the Great Mystery, having a conversation with Life can happen in uncountable ways. (In fact I was slightly blown away when the man, who had signed his name Lief, added: "pronounced Life." I'm still grinning.) It could be that we are all encouraging ourselves and one another to realize that we are indeed the Infinite and Eternal experiencing Itself.

Epilogue

Following the world-shaking event of September 11, 2001, waves of aftershock swept across this nation and around the planet. A shudder of fear, which had already begun before that morning, waking many from prophetic nightmares, caused millions of citizens to feel vulnerable and uncertain of their future. Close behind the surge of stunned apprehension flowed a wave of love and support, not only among strangers in supermarkets and employees in their workplaces, but from other countries rallying to assist and comfort this country. Into the wake of this increased cohesion tumbled a barrage of reactions, everything from outrage to the recognition of a wake-up call needed to be heeded on many levels.

And then, it seemed, at least for most of the people I was communicating with, during the winter months following the gradual process of becoming accustomed to the restless state of world affairs, a wave of personal challenges hit hard. An influx of reports of emotional and physical agony and despair, sudden deaths, diagnoses of incurable disease, shattered relationships, financial collapse, staggered me as I worked my way through my own sense of disconnection and doubt.

The spring, however, brought an equally overwhelming flood of miraculous resolutions. Someone who had been dying of leukemia recovered. A terrible custody battle shifted into a better relationship between parents and child. A job that had seemed out of reach became a life purpose. The death of a father provided a new opening to life for those he left behind. A wrenching disappointment in love became the impetus to connect with more unconditional love to self and others. A man who had seen his brothers killed in the attack on the Pentagon found a calling as a security guard in an art museum, where he took pride in reconnecting people to the enduring inspiration and beauty of culture. A Peace Forum that had barely gotten off the ground swelled into a communication with spiritually conscious members of the government.

The contractions that seemed to have reduced so many of us to the densest levels of doubt, fear, and pain before ushering us into a more connected relationship with life were much like the contractions of labor during birthing, which are painful when resisted, but exhilarating when put into the context of what is occurring, a breakthrough into new life, an expansion beyond the limits of out-dated confinement, the invisible made visible, a new sense of purpose unfolding into the future.

I've experienced many rebirths during the course of my lifetime. I have a revised understanding, since the earlier ones, of what has been happening, and will inevitably continue to happen. My spiritual growth has not been a path. It has been a succession of spherical quantum leaps into greater consciousness. Each growth period has brought me to the outer limits of my ability to live in awareness, where once again I bump into a shell of still unacknowledged prejudices, separatist definitions, unnoticed identification with this person, in this body, in this culture, more than with this fluid expression of Universal Oneness. Because I am an expression of Universal Oneness, I need the limits to know my limitlessness, I need the progression of time to know my timelessness, and so I give myself these expanding concentric spheres, I give myself the challenge of feeling too small, too cramped, too pained, too fearful, within this sphere that only recently I'd experienced as so much larger than the one in which I'd contained myself earlier in time.

Our species is doing the same thing. Never have we been so interconnected electronically, so advanced technologically, so globally aware of the basic humanness within every culture, or so insistent on taking care of one another and the planet. In some ways we are closer to global unity and harmony than we have ever been. At the same time, we have reached the invisible limits of this sphere of consciousness, and we are giving ourselves the challenge of breaking through outmoded prejudices, a narrow focus on differences, an unnecessary identification with labels instead of with the Universal Oneness of which we are all an integral part. What appears to be contractions into the density of our most debilitating human emotions -- fear, outrage, hatred, revenge, greed, arrogance -- are the contractions that shove us outward, to be bigger than the pain, free of the illusion of scarcity, open to mutual regard and nurturance, a global community long in the making and so close to emerging that signs of it are manifesting everywhere.

Listening to the conversation of two women at a dinner party, I was updated on the expanded attitudes around adoption and psychotherapy. The process of adoption, according to one of the women, which was once determined by agents to be best handled with no communication between biological parents and adoptive ones, is now a process of mediating where on the scale of relationship both parties are most comfortable, from the minimum exchange of occasional photos of the child to the active involvement of both sets of parents in the child's upbringing. Everyone affected has something to say in the matter. The patriarchal assumption that an assumed authority is best equipped to determine outcomes has dissolved into a shared responsibility. I silently cheered at this news. The other woman described her first therapy session with an eleven-year-old girl who had been so neglected and abused in an orphanage in eastern Europe that when she joined her adoptive American family at the age of seven, she couldn't tolerate being touched. Her first therapist had recommended that the parents hold her through her struggles until she subsided, but this had only exacerbated the problems. This woman had sat with the girl and asked her, "What is it that therapists do wrong?" The girl wrote out a long list. "And what is it that therapists do right?" The girl wrote out another list. Authority over the healing process had been granted to the only person who could best determine it, the client herself, and of course progress was assured. I gazed in admiration at these two women, one who is the ex-wife of the father of my once-stepchildren, and the other who is his present wife. We had come together to celebrate the birthday of an eleven-year-old boy we all consider our grandchild.

Many children of about that same age are being recognized as the next stage of human evolution. Indigo children, Crystal children, Rainbow children, Star children, these are some of the names given to these young people whose souls are intact or whose senses beyond those of the "normal" five are highly developed. James Twyman has written of his experiences with several youngsters who were gleaned from the general population by their answer to a question. A group of spiritual adepts, with the intention of bringing the children together to help them develop their gifts without the distraction of public schooling, canvassed local areas by asking each child, "What question would you like to pose to humanity?" In one form or another, each of these children offered a similar response. "If you knew you were an emissary of love, what would you be doing right now?" These young people are able to manipulate material reality, see auras, view the nighttime dreams and hear the thoughts of others. They speak eloquently on the subjects most crucial to the awakening of consciousness. They are in telepathic communication with one another, and there are countless numbers of them all around the globe.

Meanwhile, consciousness of the need for community and global harmony is active in the halls of politics. A bill was initiated on July 11, 2001, signed by 43 members of Congress, toward the establishment of a Department of Peace, which would "promote conflict prevention, non-violent intervention, mediation, and peaceful resolution of conflict" both domestically and internationally. It would "call on the intellectual and spiritual wealth of the people of the United States," further the education and training of peacemaking, and "increase media awareness of peace-building initiatives."

The angels of harmony are operative in every level of institution, in every nook and cranny of civilization.

My discussion group friends and I trotted across the street in a rural village in Pennsylvania to attend a lecture given by an Incan man who had been guided into the Amazon jungle, where a door was opened for him into the fifth dimension. Willaru shared with a group of twenty-or-so local people the teachings of the Ascended Masters. The information kept secret for centuries by the mystery schools of all cultures is being released in even the most unlikely places, all over the world.

Someday our planet, if enough of us continue to envision it with love, will be a nurturing Eden for everyone. We will all be equally authentic, respectful, regarded, and responsible. We will all be seen by the color of our light or the melody of our being. In this possible world of the future, there is no central authority. Every individual honors the self-sovereignty of every other one. There is no artificial scarcity. Every man, woman, and child is safe in every part of the world. Our global culture is one of infinite variety, freedom, recreation, and innovation. There are no limits to the magnificence we can experience.

Like refracting flashes of crystalline colors, the energies of billions of us are interacting to generate this promised realm. We promised it to ourselves. We came here to help reveal it, by being our true selves. Our true selves are miracle workers, time travelers, inner space explorers. Every one of us is a self-healer. Every one of us knows where to turn. Every one of us knows when to turn. Every one of us is as needed as we want to be, or as giving. When we look at one another, we see so much to love that we could not want anything to happen that wouldn't be the best possible for everyone involved.

In the meantime, as we are expanding our spheres of consciousness, generation after generation, we are already, always have been, always will be, One Universal Consciousness. The more of us who take the time to remember this, by listening to its reality within the silence of our atoms, within the liquid pulsing of our hearts, within the whispering of the wind in the trees, within the light of our being, the more we will know that you are me and I am you.

There are no boundaries. Nothing is ever lost. Reality is too immense for anything to get lost in it. Reality loops back on us and sends us into spirals and weaves us into wavelengths and knits us into designs, and when the designs seem to have ended, they are simply elsewhere, living themselves out until they reappear in recognizable colors at some other point in time that may or may not be noticeable within this one small glimpse of reality that we take in through our normal senses. We have senses far beyond this range, with which to perceive the weavings and the designs, but if we let ourselves know too much too soon, we would not need to be here, and we need to be here, somewhere between here and perfect, to differentiate, between self and other, between dark and light, between surrender and control, and we need to be here to merge the differences, again and again, into one comprehensive whole, the fabric of reality, randomness that is design, intention that is letting go, miracles that must be clothed in the mundane to have the impact of experience. We are, together with everything in this multiverse, Reality's experience of itself. We are its instruments, and we are its audience, we are its songwriters, and we are its songs.

Excuse me, the phone is ringing. "Hello?"
"Hello. This is God. I'm in Heaven when I'm with you."
"Oh! Wow. Okay. Thanks!"

"Gimme the phone, God. Hello, this is Allah. I'm in Heaven when I'm with you."

"Oh. Wow. Mmm. Thank you."

"Gimme the phone, Allah. Hello, this is Jehovah. I'm in Heaven when I'm with you."

"Oh. Thank you!"

"Gimme the phone, Jove. Hold on a minute, Spiderwoman. Hi there, this is Jesus. I'm in Heaven when I'm with you."

"Yeah!"

"Gimme the phone, dude. This is Isis, and I'm here to tell you..."

"I think I know what you're going to say."

"We're all here, babes, and have we got phones, mm-mm-mm! Pass the Word."

"Isis, tell me again, what exactly is the Word?"

"You're the Word. All of you. Spread yourselves around. Translate yourselves. Speak yourselves. Listen to yourselves. You are us. We're you. Oops, gotta go. Osiris just pulled a baby blanket over his head, and he's freaking out."

Edwards Brothers Malloy
Oxnard, CA USA
January 6, 2016